Christmas in Spain

Christmas in Spain expresses the country's rich cultural heritage. Handpainted plates on the walls of this communal courtyard reflect centuries of Moorish influence. The Christmas tree is a relatively new tradition borrowed from northern European neighbors.

Christmas in Spain

From World Book

World Book Encyclopedia, Inc.
a Scott Fetzer company
Chicago

Staff

Editorial director
William H. Nault

Editorial

Executive editor
Robert O. Zeleny

Senior editors
Seva Johnson
Scott Thomas

Staff editor
Mike Urban

Administrative assistant
Janet T. Peterson

Editorial assistant
Valerie Steward

Writer
Valjean McLenighan

Researcher
Kathleen Florio

Food consultants
Nancy Odell
Ina Pinkney

Art

Executive art director
William Hammond

Art director
Roberta Dimmer

Assistant art director
Joe Gound

Designer
Kristin Nelson

Photography director
John S. Marshall

Photographs editor
Sandra Ozanick

Crafts editor
Alice Dole

Product production

Executive director
Peter Mollman

Manufacturing
Joseph C. LaCount

Research and development
Henry Koval

Pre-press services
J. J. Stack

Production control
Janice M. Rossing

Film Separations
Alfred J. Mozdzen

Editorial services

Director
Susan C. Kilburg

Rights and permissions
Paul Rafferty

The editors wish to thank the many associations and private individuals in Spain and the United States who took part in developing this book. Special recognition goes to the staff of the Spanish National Tourist Office in Chicago—in particular to Cheryl Kiick and Luis González—for their enthusiasm and invaluable assistance in all phases of the project.

Special appreciation also goes to Julio Albi, Counselor of Cultural Affairs of the Spanish Embassy in Washington, D.C. For their generous advice and assistance, thanks go to Marina A. Seme and Bertha de la Mata.

Contents

Spain Gets Ready for Christmas

*The border design for this charming crèche was
inspired by a sixteenth-century Spanish silk embroidery motif.*

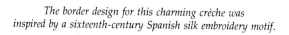

Throughout Spain, from the snowy Pyrenees to sunny Andalusia, a sense of excitement builds as the Christmas season approaches. In Spain the Christmas holidays include not one but three celebrations—Christmas Eve, Christmas Day, and the Day of the Three Kings (January 6), each with its own special customs and activities.

Spain is a country of great regional differences. On the northeastern border, the mighty mountains called the Pyrenees separate the Iberian Peninsula (which includes Spain and Portugal) from France. The southernmost tip of Spain, on the other hand, lies only about 10 miles (16 kilometers) from the northern coast of Africa, across the Strait of Gibraltar.

The official language of Spain is Castilian Spanish taught in the schools and spoken by most of the people. But in certain northern provinces, a second language is used in addition to Castilian Spanish. In Catalonia, the northeasternmost province, many people speak Catalan, a language similar to the Provençal of southern France, just over the Pyrenees. The Basque provinces in north-central Spain have their own tongue, a language with no known relations: Basque, also known as Euskera. In northwestern Galicia, a province just north of Portugal, most people speak a Portuguese dialect known as Galician.

Since climate and even language may differ markedly from one region of the country to another, it is not surprising that Christmas observances also vary considerably from region to region. Even within a particular province, Christmas customs and traditions in small towns and villages often have quite a different character and tone from activities in the larger cities.

Spaniards from the northern regions are likely to decorate their homes with mistletoe and holly as the Nativity approaches, while southerners celebrate with geraniums and heliotrope. The plant life of the two regions reflects the striking climatic difference between them. A white Christmas is not at all unusual in the Pyrenees or the mountains of Galicia in the northwest. But a Christmas snowfall in Málaga or Cádiz on the southern coast would cause quite a sensation.

The cultures of the north and south are as different as their climates. Spain lived under Moslem rule for some 700 years before Ferdinand and Is-

abella finally drove the last of the Moslem kings from Granada in 1492. For centuries the north—a center of Visigothic resistance to Moslem rule—evolved primarily under the influence of Roman/European civilizations. The southern portions of the peninsula, on the other hand, were influenced predominantly by Asiatic, Saracen cultures. Though the Saracen rulers were tolerant of Christianity, the celebration of Christmas tended to be downplayed in southern Spain.

Roman Catholicism has exerted a unifying influence over the various regions of Spain since the death of the Islamic king Boabdil. But even the strong hold of Spanish Catholicism has not obliterated regional differences in Spain.

Religious observance of the feast of the Nativity is much more rigorous in the rural areas than in the cities of Spain. Similarly, one is more likely to come across traditional and distinctly Spanish Christmas customs and practices in small towns and villages than in the bustling metropolitan centers.

Spain is gradually adopting more and more American and northern European Christmas customs, especially in the large cities and among the

In some parts of the high Pyrenees, especially along the Spanish-French border, Christmas snows make the mountains so impassable that the Nativity is celebrated on February 2, the Feast of Candlemas.

*Her Christmas turkey in hand, this Spanish
housewife turns her attention to ingredients for the stuffing.*

well-to-do. This development probably reflects the
rapid economic expansion that has transformed
Spain from a poor farming country into an indus-
trial nation in the last two or three decades.

Occasionally, one may see a Santa Claus roam-
ing the streets of Madrid, Barcelona, or one of the
other major cities. Although the idea of Santa as a
Christmas gift bringer is now fairly widespread in
urban Spain, his presence in the pre-Christmas
season is not nearly so universal as it is in the
United States.

Traditionally, the Three Kings are the ones who
delight Spanish children with holiday presents. In
the old days, gifts were exchanged exclusively on
Three Kings' Day (January 6) and were intended
primarily for the children. Today the exchange of
gifts at Christmastime is becoming increasingly
common among urban Spaniards.

Traditional Christmas wreaths decorate the
doors of many Spanish homes. Candles, branches
of holly, and other Christmas greenery are also
typical.

Many city families have adopted the custom of
putting up a Christmas tree—a practice that originated in northern Europe. Almost all city people
live in apartments, and it is quite common to
place the family tree outdoors on the apartment
balcony rather than inside. Large condominium
complexes will often erect a huge community tree,
decorated with electric lights, in the common outdoor courtyard area.

Early in December, outdoor Christmas markets
begin to appear in the larger cities. In Madrid, for
example, trees and Christmas ornaments are sold
in the Plaza Mayor. Completed in 1620 during the
reign of Philip III, this historic square has served
as the site of bullfights, masked balls, fireworks
displays, the burning of heretics, and the canon-
ization of several saints. In the summer the Plaza
Mayor hosts occasional theatrical performances.
But around December 1, the ancient cobblestones
ring with the sounds of merchants setting up their
stalls for the holiday season.

The typical Spanish Christmas market is a riot
of color. Christmas ornaments of every size,
shape, and hue compete for the shoppers' attention, as well as for their *pesetas* (money). Some of
the stalls feature row upon row of colored plastic
balls—the most prevalent decoration by far, and
certainly among the cheapest. Stars for the treetop
twinkle and glitter next to colorful garlands of tinsel. One vendor might specialize in shiny ribbons
for decorating trees and tying up holiday packages. Another might offer lovely handmade ornaments of wood or straw.

The American influence is easy to spot on shelf
after shelf of Santa Claus figures and strings of

The purchase of a Christmas tree involves youngsters and grownups alike, at least in the major cities. Vendors drive a hard bargain.

electric lights. Inexpensive toys of almost every description are imported from many other countries as well.

The markets also sell supplies for making *nacimientos* or *belenes* (Bethlehems), the crèches or Nativity scenes that are found in almost every Spanish home at Christmastime. There are sheets of cork for constructing a stable or cave, and moss on which tiny sheep or camels can graze. Miniature figures of the Holy Family, the Three Kings, and animals of every description abound.

A visit to a Spanish Christmas market is a delight for the senses. Besides the profusion of colors and sights, the scent of evergreens adds to the holiday spirit. Christmas wreaths, branches of pine and holly, and pine and fir trees of every size are available for sale. It is common to find gypsies selling Christmas trees in the markets, and a good deal of haggling generally goes on before buyer and seller agree to a price. But the cacophony of offers and counteroffers is all in good fun and only serves to punctuate the holiday mood.

As Christmas Eve draws closer, Spanish cooks begin to turn their fancy to the culinary delights they will prepare for family and friends. Spanish cuisine is as varied from region to region as is the climate, the language, and the many customs. There is no surer way to ignite an argument among a group of Spaniards than to ask for an "authentic" recipe for *paella*, the delightful saffron-

9

Shopping areas in the larger cities lure customers in the weeks before Christmas with giant communal Christmas trees and a blaze of electric lights.

flavored rice dish that is one of the hallmarks of Spanish cuisine. Each region has its own special way of preparing paella, and each can rightly claim to have an "authentic" recipe.

There are a few other dishes that a visitor to Spain can reasonably expect to find almost anyplace in the country. Flan (a caramel custard) and spongecake are available in most restaurants, and one form or another of garlic soup can be found in every farmhouse from Córdoba to Bilbao. But each area has its own way of preparing these foods and often wrinkles its nose at the way certain dishes are cooked in neighboring provinces. The Andalusians dislike the Catalan taste for sweets with meats, and the Catalans, in turn, find the peppery food of the Estremadurans thoroughly disagreeable. One food writer summed up the argument by dubbing Spanish cooking a "regional cuisine with national characteristics."

In rural areas, the smell of roasting chestnuts tempts homeward-bound villagers during the pre-Christmas season. Vendors stick close to their braziers for warmth.

Despite regional differences, there are certain foods that are customarily served at Christmastime in almost every part of Spain. One of these is roast turkey or, in certain areas, roast capon. Although it originated in the Americas, the fowl that helped the Pilgrims through their first few winters is by no means an exclusively American favorite. The turkey made its European debut in Spain sometime during the sixteenth century, courtesy of the conquistadors, who brought a few turkeys back from Mexico to astonish the Spanish court. The bird's popularity quickly spread from the New World to the Old. By the eighteenth century the turkey was the "monarch of the Christmas table" in many parts of Europe, including Spain. As the poet John Gay wrote: "From the low peasant to the lord, the turkey smokes on every board."

In many parts of Spain, as the winter solstice approaches, thousands of turkeys appear as if by magic to flood the market—or, in some areas, literally to overrun the market. In Seville, for example, it is still the custom for turkey farmers to drive flocks of gobblers through the streets, while householders look on from open doors and windows. Discriminating shoppers look for the fattest, most succulent toms and hens and sometimes take the birds home live for extra fattening before they are slaughtered.

Spanish cooks, like Americans, generally stuff their birds before roasting. But Spaniards use breadcrumbs only as a means of holding or binding the rest of the ingredients together, not as the basis of the stuffing. Most American recipes call for considerably larger amounts of breadcrumbs or cracker crumbs than a Spanish cook would find palatable. As for the rest of the ingredients, there are almost as many recipes for Spanish stuffing as there are Spanish cooks. Most make use of two staples, the basic elements of Spanish cuisine: olive oil and garlic. These have been used in Spain since Roman troops occupied the country. Many recipes call for some sort of pork—bacon, chunks of ham, or often pork sausage. Onions are a common ingredient, as are mushrooms and, for those who can afford them, truffles. Chestnuts or pine nuts are also popular. Recipes that call for fresh or dried fruit—apples, oranges, dried apricots, prunes, and raisins—are modern-day reminders that the Moorish influence on Spanish culture is still very much alive.

Spaniards frequently bone their turkey before stuffing and roasting. The bird is basted with olive oil or butter and lemon juice, or sometimes with an orange sauce like that used for duck. The turkey comes to the table looking much like a shiny, golden football, ready to be carved and served.

Felices Pascuas ("Happy Holiday") or *Felices Pascuas de Navidad* (literally, "Happy Holiday of the Nativity") is the standard greeting of one Spaniard to another as Christmas Eve approaches. In the larger cities, streets and major squares are gaily decorated with electric lights and other ornaments. Department stores display their wares beneath banners expressing that most universal of Christmas sentiments: *Paz en la Tierra a los Hombres de Buena Voluntad*—Peace on Earth to People of Good Will.

El Cant dels Ocells
(Carol of the Birds)

Upon this holy night,
When God's great star appears,
And floods the earth with brightness,
Birds' voices rise in song,
And, warbling all night long,
Express their glad hearts' lightness.

The Nightingale is first
To bring his song of cheer,
And tell us of his gladness:
"Jesus, our Lord, is born
To free us from all sin,
And banish ev'ry sadness."

The answ'ring Sparrow cries:
"God comes to earth this day
Amid the angels flying."
Trilling in sweetest tones,
The Finch his Lord now owns:
"To Him be all thanksgiving."

The Partidge adds his note:
"To Bethlehem I'll fly,
Where in the stall He's lying.
There, near the manger blest,
I'll build myself a nest,
And sing my love undying."

Tradespeople commonly send Christmas cards to valued clients. The card on the right contains greetings from the distributor of Barcelona's daily La Vanguardia.

The excitement of the approaching festivities is just as great in the rural areas. Instead of electric Christmas lights, the warm glow of charcoal braziers illuminates village footpaths as chestnut vendors roast their wares for homebound shepherds, farmers, and shopkeepers.

No significant event takes place in Spain without being celebrated in song and dance—least of all *la Navidad,* or Christmas. As one might expect, there is as much variety in costume, music, and styles of dancing from region to region as there is in climate and cuisine. One generalization that can be made, however, is that the celebration of Christmas in rural areas is more deeply religious in character than in the larger cities. Take, for example, "El Cant dels Ocells," a carol that originated in Catalonia and has become one of the most popular in Spain. The "Carol of the Birds"

Women in a Toledo candy shop mold marzipan into Christmas treats. This delicious sugar and almond confection is a legacy of the Moorish occupation of Spain.

tells the story of the Nativity from the point of view of the birds that witnessed the event. Like the shepherd from whose imagination they sprang, the birds in the carol are clearly well versed in the Catholic faith.

The custom of exchanging Christmas cards is common both in rural and urban areas. The cards typically feature reproductions of paintings of the Nativity or Three Kings, though in larger cities it is possible to purchase cards with more secular holiday graphics and greetings.

In certain areas, various service and tradespeople will present cards—similar to calling cards—to their customers with greetings such as, "Your postal worker wishes you a Happy Holiday Season." In return, the customer presents a cash gift. One travel writer describes a traffic cop in Ávila on the day before Christmas enclosed in a waist-high wall of hams, cheeses, fruits, and wineskins—all presents from the good citizens of his district.

Large commercial organizations—banks, corporations, and the like—often send huge, elaborate baskets of liquor, fruit, and sweets to important clients. Shops and delis in the larger cities sometimes feature these baskets in display windows. Curious shoppers enjoy looking the baskets over, but they are not the sort of present a self-respecting Spaniard would give to a friend or relative.

Among the many sweets available in Spain at Christmastime, none is molded into more fantastic guises than marzipan, an Arabic delicacy which the Spanish know as *mazapán*. Made of crushed almonds (a gift of the Moslems), plus sugar and eggs, Spanish marzipan has such distinctive qualities that many say it is the best in the world.

Toledo is the marzipan capital of Spain. The city is as well-known for its sweets as it is for the keen blades it produces for bullfighting. The nuns of the convent of Jesús y María have been making mazapán for generations, as have numerous family-owned businesses.

The Christmas market in Madrid's Plaza Mayor
attracts crowds of shoppers looking for nacimiento
figures. Each year Spanish artisans reaffirm the
durability of the handcrafted tradition.

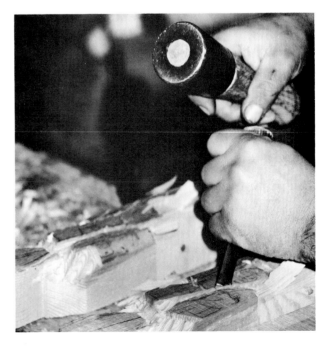

Connoisseurs of Spanish marzipan can discuss its fine points for hours on end. Do the best almonds come from Andalusia in the south? Yes, say some. Others, however, insist that the finest almonds in the world come from south of Valencia, along the Mediterranean coast.

Spanish marzipan can be shaped into balls, or ovals, or sometimes into little cups and filled with apricot jam. But at Christmastime Toledo's masters and mistresses of mazapán let their imaginations run wild. The candy is formed into utterly fantastic shapes. Long lengths of mazapán are coiled into round boxes and decorated to look like eels or dragons. With sugar scales, candy eyes, and almond-studded jaws, these toothsome monsters are shipped all over Spain, and as far as *América del Norte*, to delight and amaze children of all ages.

In every house in Spain—poor or rich, but especially those where children are living—the universal pre-Christmas activity is the construction and erection of the family *nacimiento*, the Nativity scene. Many families buy the necessary figures, but most make their own setting—a cave or stable, and a background that may be as simple as shepherds on a hillside or as elaborate as a re-creation of the entire town of Bethlehem. Children and adults alike spend much time on this family project.

A typical family nacimiento will include the figures of Mary, Joseph, and the infant Jesus, plus the Three Kings, some shepherds, and an angel announcing the birth of Christ. These are the basics. Many nacimientos, however, are much more elaborate. The Kings' entourage may feature a number of servants, plus camels, donkeys, or whatever transportation the family decides befits such a royal party. A river of aluminum foil is a common background feature, with one or more women doing laundry and perhaps a couple of people fishing. Some nacimientos even include the castle of King Herod and the figures of Roman soldiers.

At urban Christmas markets, one can purchase entire families of miniature animals to place in the nacimiento—sow and piglets, cow and calf, hen and chicks, and more. With so many city families living in small apartments, most urban nacimientos are scaled to fit a compact space. But in larger homes or public places, nacimientos may be much larger, even life-sized.

Some schools and churches have living nacimientos—*tableaux vivants*. Students or parishioners assume the various roles in the Nativity scene. Some groups use nacimientos as fundraising vehicles. An orphanage in Madrid with a particularly elaborate nacimiento charges admission to view the display. The money is used to support the orphanage.

Belenistas are clubs or organizations devoted to building and admiring nacimientos. The groups organize displays and sometimes competitions in which awards are given to the best nacimiento in a particular year.

As the Advent season draws to a close, Spaniards exchange holiday greetings, busy themselves with the family nacimiento, and otherwise prepare for Christmas Eve, fully savoring the pleasure of anticipation. Along city streets and village lanes, spirits rise as steadily as the Christmas star.

A Spanish Christmas: Revelry and Reverence

*Reverent shepherds grace the façade of Barcelona's
Temple of the Holy Family, designed by Antonio Gaudí.*

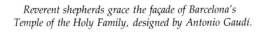

Christmas in Spain is a festival that blends the religious spirit of the Nativity with the delights of the table, and the Spanish passion for song and dance with the universal pleasure of renewing family ties. The Spanish Christmas Eve is known as *Noche buena,* the "good night." It is a time of gaiety and merrymaking. Early in the day, everyone who can do so hurries forth into the streets. In cities and villages people browse through the markets for last-minute purchases of food, decorations, and, increasingly, presents.

In village markets, turkeys that escaped Advent grocery shopping gobble forlornly from stacked cages. Quacking ducks and cooing pigeons help to swell the sounds of Christmas. Towering piles of golden Valencia oranges, luscious dates, and olives, which are indispensable to any Spanish feast, threaten to overwhelm display shelves. Scattered among them are cheeses of every conceivable variety, quaint pigskins of wine, and choice candies from many parts of Spain.

Every region seems to have its own sweetmeat or pastry specialty. In all but the smallest towns and villages, however, *pastelerias* and tearooms offer an extraordinary variety of *dulces* (sweets): plump, sugar-coated fruits; cream- or custard-filled cakes; and pastries oozing with jam.

Pineapples from the Azores, bananas from the Canary Islands, juicy melons, oranges, pears, plums, and other fresh fruits are the usual mealtime desserts in Spain. Still, there seems to be a constant demand for dulces, and no more so than at Christmastime.

Over a cup of tea, coffee, or the thick, rich chocolate that is so popular in Spain, the Iberian woman takes time out from preparing for the onslaught of distant relatives to relish a dainty cake or pastry and wish her sisters the joys of the season. The tearoom is to the Spanish woman what the all-male cafe is to her husband—a place to congregate between lunch and dinner and share the events of the day with friends.

The universal Christmas treat in Spain is *turrón,* a kind of nougat made with toasted almonds, sugar, honey, and eggs. Like many traditional Spanish foods, this one comes in a variety of guises. Some forms simply melt in one's mouth; others have the consistency of peanut brittle, hard and almost rocklike.

Under the watchful eye of his father, a Madrid youngster tries out a pandereta, *or tambourine, for use in the Christmas Eve revels.*

Turrón is eaten by poor and rich alike in Spain, and it is a point of honor to buy it when it is offered for sale at one's door. It comes in several qualities and prices.

Historians differ in their accounts of the origin of this universal Spanish treat. Some trace the tradition back a thousand years before the time of Christ, when Carthaginians came to the Iberian Peninsula from Asia Minor. They used to offer gifts in the form of cakes to one of their goddesses, the Lady Baalat. The custom later evolved into a kind of ritual consumption: "Take ye and eat."

Other historians suggest that the giving of turrón may harken back to the Roman custom of exchanging sweetmeats at the January calends, to ensure that the coming year might be full of sweetness. But no matter how the custom began, absolutely everyone in Spain buys and eats turrón at Christmastime.

Regional favorites also play an important role in satisfying the Spanish sweet tooth during the Christmas holidays. In rural Aragon, an almond caramel called *guirlache* is a popular way to top off the Noche buena meal. Various sections of the Asturias are famous for their tarts. *Escaldau*, made from corn, rye flour, honey and butter, is served steaming hot, fresh from the oven. *Quesadillas*, stuffed with cheese, fruit, or sometimes nuts, are another Asturian favorite.

Although the Iberians are justly famous for their hospitality, the Noche buena meal, and the Christmas meal as well, are generally reserved for the immediate and extended family. There are other occasions during the holidays that Spaniards share with friends—notably New Year's Eve. But Christmas is almost exclusively a family affair.

The traditional Noche buena dinner is quite an elaborate meal, consisting of several courses. Menus vary from province to province, of course, but there are certain recurring themes in many Spanish homes.

As likely as not, visiting relatives will be welcomed by the scent of freshly roasted chestnuts, a fragrance that punctuates the Spanish holidays from Noche buena all the way through Three Kings' Day. The chestnut grows well in Spain and is a favorite with Spanish palates. Toasted almonds are another popular appetizer, as are olives that have been marinated for several days in olive oil and garlic. The first course is often rounded out by a selection of fine cheeses, perhaps accompanied by anchovies. In homes that can afford it, all is washed down with a glass or two of muscatel or Spanish sherry.

Chestnut soup—or a creamy almond soup that is as delicate as angels' wings—is an optional second course. Whether or not a soup is prepared, most households offer a fish course before bringing out the holiday turkey.

One of the most traditional Christmas dishes is *besugo*, a Mediterranean sea bream very similar to American red snapper. In places where bream is not available, Spanish cooks often substitute flounder. The fish is topped with seasoned breadcrumbs, lightly sprinkled with olive oil, and baked whole, often surrounded by sliced potatoes and onions. Garnished with lemon slices, besugo makes an attractive addition to the holiday table. In Galicia the fish course is *bacalao*, made from the dried salt codfish so plentiful in that region. First the fish is tenderized by beating it against a tabletop. Then it must be soaked in water at least overnight. The prepared fish is dusted with flour and fried in olive oil with potatoes and onions. The finished creation is brought to the table crowned with parsley and olives and garnished with slices of hard-cooked egg.

Substitutions for the traditional Christmas turkey abound. In Galicia a suckling pig or meat pie might be served; while in rural Aragon, the Christmas Eve meal might include a main course of lamb and chicken. There are also regional variations on turkey. *Madrilenos*, that is, the citizens of Madrid, frequently accompany their Christmas turkey with a side dish of red cabbage—*Lombarda de San Isidro*. Curiously enough, the dish is named for San Isidro, the city's patron saint. Green beans in tomato sauce is another popular favorite. Fresh green beans are lightly sautéed in olive oil and garlic, combined with chopped tomatoes and pine nuts, and seasoned with lemon juice and bay leaf.

The standard way to top off a Noche buena meal is with a big, rectangular block of turrón. The block is cut into individual slices for serving. Candy-coated almonds may also be offered, as well as a compote of apples, pears, or mixed fruits.

The dessert is accompanied by champagne or some other wine. Catalonia produces champagne, so this sparkling beverage is within the means of most Spanish families. In those humble homes where it is not, the hosts generally substitute a sparkling cider.

Having carefully scrutinized the morning's catch, a housewife pays for her besugo, *or sea bream, the traditional fish course for the Christmas meal.*

The Noche buena meal is, obviously, quite a production, and there always seems to be some forgotten ingredient or other that has to be purchased at the last minute. As Christmas Eve shoppers hurry through the afternoon sun, they are sped on their way by the sound of guitars, castanets, and other traditional folk instruments. On every other corner, it seems, groups of musicians gather to perform the traditional Spanish carols known as *villancicos.* As often as not, people who pause to listen for a moment or two will join in the refrain.

One noteworthy Christmas Eve tradition in Spain is the practice of granting amnesty to military and political prisoners and criminals. On or just before Noche buena, prison officials make the rounds of their wards, accompanied by lawyers. Prisoners whose offenses seem reasonably pardonable are set free, in the spirit of the season.

Perhaps in memory of Mary and Joseph, who had no one to care for them in their time of need, many Spaniards make a point of going to a hospital on Christmas Eve and visiting the sick—whether or not they are relatives. And for centuries it was the custom in Spain to place a lighted oil lamp in a window as soon as dusk fell on Christmas Eve. Many families, especially those living in the countryside, still follow this practice. Religious families may also light candles before the home shrine to the Virgin Mary or place candles around the family nacimiento.

The influence of the original Spanish settlers is still apparent in certain parts of the southwestern United States, where the practice of setting out *luminarios* (festive lights) on Christmas Eve persists. Luminarios are made by partly filling paper bags with sand and inserting a candle in each bag. The luminarios are placed on rooftops, garden walls, and walkways. They are lighted at dusk on Christmas Eve, and the soft, radiant light is said to guide the Christ child to each home.

After nightfall in Spanish households, aunts, uncles, brothers, sisters, grandparents, and cousins galore begin to arrive. The walls reverberate with the noisy chatter that is typical of

*Shoppers at this Christmas market can select from among
a small army of miniature* nacimiento *figures.*

most family reunions. The children grow more
and more impatient as the house fills with the
tempting smells of the Noche buena dinner.
Around nine or ten—not an unusual dinner hour
in Spain—the family sits down to eat, and the
meal continues until it is time for midnight mass.

The *Misa del gallo*, or mass of the cock's crow, is
the only mass said at midnight the whole year-
round. And for the little ones especially, it has an
air of great excitement and adventure. Many of
them have never before been out so late.

In small towns, everyone will turn out for the
midnight mass, which is a social, as well as a religious, event. People who have moved away frequently travel many miles from their homes in the
larger cities to attend Christmas Eve mass at their
native village churches. Everyone in town is curious to see who will show up—and with whom—
what new babies have been born, and so on.

Although in big cities, social pressure to attend

mass is much less intense, midnight mass on
Christmas Eve is still a widespread custom. For
this special occasion, priests put on their most
gorgeous robes, some of them worn only on
Christmas Eve. The vestments are adorned with
rare embroidery, and they sparkle with precious
jewels. In the great cathedrals, the rich tones of
the organ swell along with the music from guitars,
tambourines, and castanets. Priests, choir, and
congregation join to sing traditional carols.

The celebration of the midnight mass in La-
bastida, the province of Alava, dates from the
Middle Ages. Just before midnight, in front of the
Consistorial House, a dozen shepherds gather to
sing some songs for the mayor and town council.
Led by an old man carrying a lamb, and a shepherdess bearing an image of the infant Jesus, the
group sings all the way to church. There they
greet the priest and perform a ritual dance that involves beating the floor with sticks. There is singing and dancing all through the mass. Afterward,
the shepherds build a bonfire near the church and

In Malago, a youngster stands spellbound before a display of shiny new Christmas decorations.

pretend to make some soup, which is offered to the Christ child, still safe in the arms of the shepherdess.

Even though the thermometer may register below freezing, in Burgos shepherds celebrate the traditional midnight mass in the open air, near the Shepherds Monument. The starlight ceremony, overlooking the Castile plains, is incomparable.

In the Pyrenees, rural folk remember the dead on Christmas Eve. There, it is the custom to leave out a loaf of bread with a knife stuck in it before going off to midnight mass. The loaf has been left as food for the dead.

After church on Christmas Eve, most Spaniards return home and go to sleep. Some, however, continue their Christmas Eve merrymaking until the wee hours of the morning. Gypsy dancers are happy to accommodate their fellow night owls with songs and dances that have been passed on from generation to generation. One traditional lyric sums up the spirit of the occasion: "Long live merrymaking, for this is a day of rejoicing. And

may the perfume of pleasure sweeten our existence."

Gift giving on either Christmas Eve or the morning of Christmas Day is becoming more and more customary in urban Spain. Some upper-class families even follow the northern European custom of hanging stockings on the mantle. Santa Claus is the bearer of these Christmas gifts—for the adults as well as for the youngsters. Families caught in this cultural crossfire have to figure out for themselves how to divide their gift giving between Christmas and Three Kings' Day, the traditional and still universal Spanish holiday for the exchange of presents.

On Christmas morning, the family nacimiento becomes the center of attention. The figure of the Christ child is lovingly put into place in the manger scene, and the crib is illuminated by candlelight. The children, often dressed in peasant costumes and playing tambourines, castanets, and

Busy shoppers take time out for a moment to enjoy a villancico, *or traditional Christmas carol, performed by street musicians.*

Traditional Spanish [GKE]

Traditional Spanish [WE]

Come, My Dear Old Lady
(Ya Viene la Vieja)

2. Kings of Orient riding,
Cross the sandy desert,
Bringing for the Baby
Wine and cookies sweet.
    Refrain

3. Kings of Orient riding,
Guided by the starlight,
Bringing to the Baby
Gifts of love, this night.
    Refrain

other traditional folk instruments, sing and dance to the lilting strains of Spanish villancicos. Once the children have had their chance to perform, everyone joins in singing the beloved carols.

What the Christmas tree is to northern Europe, the nativity scene is to the south. This Christmas custom is said to have originated in the Middle Ages, and its popularization is most often ascribed to Saint Francis of Assisi, the "Little Brother of Mankind."

During the Middle Ages there were few books and few people able to read. Masses and church ceremonies were conducted in Latin, and Saint Francis worried, with good reason, that important holidays such as Christmas and Easter held little real meaning for the common folk. It was his earnest desire to humanize the teachings of the Scriptures, to help ordinary people feel a deeper religious experience by making sacred truths more accessible.

Legend has it that Saint Francis was inspired to set up a nativity scene when he saw some shepherds asleep in the fields near Greccio, Italy. It occurred to him that a live reenactment of the arrival

Stuffing the Christmas turkey and grinding the almonds for sopa de almendra—*methods have changed since the nineteenth century, but not the Christmas menu.*

of the Savior would help to make the true significance of the Nativity apparent to all.

Before making his plans, Saint Francis went to Rome to secure permission from the pope. With the consent of Honorius III in hand, Saint Francis turned to a wealthy nobleman, Giovanni of Greccio, for assistance.

The event took place in a cave on a hill above Greccio. Giovanni's comings and goings created quite a stir in the town and countryside. The nobleman hired real persons to take the parts of Mary, Joseph, and the shepherds, and he commissioned a life-sized wax figure to represent the Christ child. When all the properties had been assembled, including a manger, straw, a live ox, and a donkey, Saint Francis himself arranged and directed the scene.

On Christmas Eve, 1223, throngs of worshipers crowded the hillside, many carrying torches and presents for the Holy Infant. Saint Bonaventure described the scene in his biography of Saint Francis, published 40 years later. Many witnesses, Bonaventure said, came to understand the meaning of the birth in Bethlehem for the first time. Saint Francis was so delighted that he stood before the manger "bathed in tears and overflowing with joy."

On Christmas Eve and Christmas Day, families traditionally share elaborate dinners, seasoned with good holiday spirit.

Saint Francis celebrated a solemn mass and preached a sermon to the audience. He begged them to cleanse their hearts of hatred and to entertain only thoughts of peace during the Christmas season. He also sought to underscore the meaning of the Nativity by pointing out that the Christ child, Savior of the world, was just as poor as, if not poorer than, the assembled worshipers.

Francis's dramatization made such an impression on the people of Greccio that the practice was repeated Christmas after Christmas. Soon it spread throughout Italy, and from there to Spain, Portugal, France, and the rest of Europe.

The saint led his people in songs of joy. No doubt some of these songs were among the earliest Christmas carols. He encouraged the children who were present to sing around the manger to the Baby Jesus. From this custom have come several beautiful lullabies to the Christ child, including a few of the oldest villancicos. And, of course, the modern practice of singing and dancing around the nacimiento can be traced directly to the event at Greccio.

Having concluded their devotions at home, many devout Spanish Catholic families attend one or more of the three masses that are offered on Christmas Day. The main meal of the day is taken around the middle of the afternoon and, like the Noche buena dinner, is shared with members of the extended family. The Christmas dinner is generally as elaborate as the previous day's, with a main course of roast turkey, goose, or capon. *Puchero olla*—a special dish made of chicken, beef, mutton, bacon, pig's feet, and garlic—may also be featured. The meal is washed down with plenty of wine—Spanish families reserve their best vintages for the holiday season—and topped off with the everpresent turrón.

The traditional rite of the Urn of Fate is a practice that has survived since the days when Roman troops occupied the Iberian Peninsula. In many communities, the names of friends and neighbors are written on cards and placed in a giant bowl. With much laughter and merriment, the cards are drawn two at a time, to see who fate has determined must become special friends during the following year.

In some communities, this old folkway is a kind of matchmaking ceremony, and names in the bowl may be shamelessly maneuvered by interested parties to achieve the desired results. The outcome is sometimes disappointing, but everyone grins and bears it.

Youngsters in Cádiz perform another rite that dates from pagan times, "swinging the sun."

At midnight on Christmas Eve, Spaniards flock to mass to join the priest and choir in welcoming the newborn Christ child.

Swings are set up in the public squares, and the children compete to see who can go highest in the air, thus helping the sun on its return journey northward. The custom is a modern-day reminder that the feast of Christmas has its origins in ancient celebrations of the winter solstice.

Catalonian villagers have their own colorful ways of celebrating the Christmas holidays. Young boys of the village traditionally get together on Christmas Day to drag a Yule log through the streets, beating it soundly, to ensure good luck in the coming year. The boys drag the log from door to door, and at every house where they stop they are given presents of nuts and candies.

Another variation of this theme is the Catalonian practice of hanging up a hollow log, or *tio*, for Christmas. The log is lovingly covered with burlap and trimmed with gifts for the youngsters. Inside the trunk, more gifts are crammed. On Christmas Day the children laughingly beat the log with sticks, and the goodies come tumbling forth.

In the shadow of the Pyrenees, Christmas is traditionally celebrated with song. Groups of carolers are called *Rosers*—members of the Confraternity of Our Lady of the Rosary. In some villages they elect *mayorales*, whose terms last for a year from Christmas Day. These unofficial "officials" go from house to house performing traditional Christmas chants. At each door they are presented with a fresh egg for their trouble.

The Rosers may also elect priors and prioresses for one-year terms. These functionaries play an important role in the social life of the village. They attend all the weddings, baptisms, and funerals, and they are responsible for organizing and leading the village dances, as well as raising money for their Patron Lady and the church.

In some parts of the Pyrenees, young boys and girls go wassailing at homes where children have been born during the year. Chestnuts and apples are expected as rewards for their performance. If any household is foolish enough to withhold payment, the children add a final, punitive stanza to their song, hoping that the new baby will be "twisted like a pig's tail, stupid as a wooden shoe!"

By the close of Christmas Day, the newborn Christ child has been royally welcomed throughout Spain, according to the custom in each region. Family ties have been renewed, and the joys of the Nativity celebrated by sharing the finest available food and wine.

But the festivities are not yet over. For the children, especially, the best is yet to come as they look forward with mounting impatience to the arrival of the Three Kings.

Catalan children use these miniature Yule logs, or tion, *as noisemakers during their Christmas revels.*

Spanish Nativity scenes come in all sizes, including
life-sized and even larger than life. In certain areas it
is customary for live actors to portray the Holy
Family and assorted visitors.

Traditional Catalonian Carol [GKE] Traditional Catalonian Carol [WE]

1. ¡Vein - ti - cin - co de di - ciem - bre, Fum, fum, fum!
1. On De - cem - ber five and twen - ty, Foom, foom, foom!

¡Vein - ti - cin - co de di - ciem - bre, Fum, fum,
On De - cem - ber five and twen - ty, Foom, foom,

fum! Na - ci - do ha por nues - tro a - mor, El Ni - ño
foom! For the love of us is giv'n The ho - ly

Dios, el Ni - ño Dios; Hoy de la vir - gen Ma -
In - fant, Son of Heav'n, Of the Vir - gin, Jo - seph's

ri - a En es - ta no - che tan fri - a, ¡Fum, fum, fum!
bride, To all the earth good will be - tid - ing, Foom, foom, foom!

2. Little birds from out the forest,
Foom, foom, foom!
Little birds from out the forest,
Foom, foom, foom!
All your fledglings leave behind,
And seek the infant Savior kind.
Come, and build a downy nest
To warm the lovely Baby blessed,
Foom, foom, foom!

3. Little stars up in the heavens,
Foom, foom, foom!
Little stars up in the heavens,
Foom, foom, foom!
If you see the Baby cry,
O, do not answer with a sigh!
Rather, lighten up the sky
With Heav'n's beams of radiant brightness,
Foom, foom, foom!

Foom, Foom, Foom
(Fum, Fum, Fum)

The Songs and Dances
of Spanish Christmas

These lively nacimiento figures were created by the
Catalan sculptor Ramón Amadeu (1745–1821).

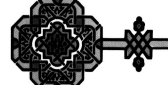

Regional folk songs and dances add a special touch to the Christmas season in Spain. As one might expect, the celebration of the Nativity in song and dance varies as much from province to province as does the Spanish climate and cuisine. Yet the love of pageantry and music is nationwide—with roots that, in many instances, can be traced back to the late Middle Ages.

Christianity was the dominant cultural force throughout Spain and western Europe from roughly 1100 to 1500. The late Middle Ages saw the spread of a wide variety of Christmas celebrations through all levels of society. Glorious masses were held in the impressive Gothic cathedrals, built as monuments to the religious fervor of kings and artists. Simpler, pious pageants, reflecting the humbler faith of the common people, were also staged in abundance.

The celebration of Christmas had its secular side as well—a side that grew in gaiety and abandon as the period progressed. The feast of the Nativity was marked with organized horseplay among ordinary citizens and ritual contests held by plumed and armor-coated knights. Riotous processions and elaborate pantomimes were capped by noisy songfests.

Christmas carols first appeared in western Europe during the late Middle Ages. Stately Christmas hymns, sung in Latin, had graced Nativity masses for centuries. These solemn verses, however, focused on the theological implications of the Incarnation. The carols, expressing the simple human emotion of joy at the birth of a Savior, were distinctly different.

The first carols were simple, homely verses set to dance tunes, which until the 1300's had been secular in theme, celebrating love, courtship, the joys of spring, or other cheerful subject matter. Beginning around 1400, Spanish and other western European composers began to adapt these secular dancing songs for religious purposes—specifically, to express the popular belief and joy in humanity's salvation, which lies at the heart of Christmas. Many Spanish carols that are still sung today had their origins in this movement, and date from the fifteenth and sixteenth centuries.

Throughout this period, the gaiety and abandonment of the Christmas holidays increased. Those who could afford to dressed and dined lav-ishly. By the mid-1400's, Spaniards were dancing in churches as well as in the streets—a practice that persists to this day.

The *tuna* are inheritors of this centuries-old tradition. These bands of university students sing and play music for the entertainment and the pesetas of holiday tourists. Their festive *traje,* or costume, has remained the same for hundreds of years: black velvet doublet, knee breeches, cloak if the weather is chilly, white neck-ruff or collar, and long, gaily colored ribbons.

The Spanish word *tuna,* literally translated, means an idle or wicked way of life, and today's young musicians do their best to live up to their name. They are just as likely to tangle with the local boys, in the traditional rivalry of town and gown, as were their forbears. To see them lustily singing in a hotel lobby, shaking their tambourines for contributions from the guests, is to travel back in history. Their appetites are truly

University students in traditional garb entertain visitors in the Malago City Hall with lively villancicos, *as Spanish students have done for centuries.*

This tenth-century, pre-Gregorian manuscript from the Cathedral of León is one of the oldest Christmas hymns.

astounding. Though generally offered wine and cakes by each establishment they visit, they seem as ravenous at the end of each evening as they were at the beginning.

Yet another group of young men who take pride in continuing a centuries-old tradition are the youngsters who perform the famous Dance of the Sixes at the cathedral in Seville. This impressive ceremony, which takes place at the close of day on December 8, the Feast of the Immaculate Conception, is a fitting beginning to the Spanish Christmas holidays. Flags fly in the streets, flowers bedeck apartment balconies, and candles are lighted in windows throughout the city.

As the afternoon sun washes the streets of Seville with an orange-pink glow, people from all over Spain, and from many foreign countries, begin to assemble in the cathedral. The Dance of the Sixes will be performed by ten choirboys before the main altar. (Although the number of participants has been expanded to ten, the dance is still known by its original name.)

The choirboys are dressed in the fashion of seventeenth-century page boys, a costume of pale blue satin trimmed in lace, complete with plumed, wide-brimmed hats. The low afternoon sun illuminates the cathedral's immense rose windows and casts long, oblique shadows across the

*The spectacular Dance of the Sixes in Seville
inaugurates the Christmas season in that city.*

ancient stone floor. Banks of candles flicker from the silver high altar, creating a glowing aura. It is a Rembrandt-like setting, rich in light and shadow.

Since dancing in all its forms is so much a part of the life and spirit of the Spanish people, this stunning and reverent ceremony is as natural as it is memorable. The ceremony begins with a simple hymn, sung by the choirboys to the accompaniment of organ and orchestra:

Hay, Jesús mío,
to amor me inflame;
Hay, hay, Jesús mío,
tu amor me inflame;
Pues ha salido para inflamarme!
Ven, amor mío;
ven, y no tardes;
ven como sueles a consolarme!

*Oh, my Jesus,
Your love inflames me.
Surely you have come to inspire me.
Come, precious Lord;
Come, don't delay;
Come, be my source
Of consolation.*

As the dance actually begins, the hymn is repeated.

The movements of the Dance of the Sixes have been compared with those of many other dances—ranging from the minuet to the performances of Japanese geishas. But the dance is, in fact, unique. Imbued with the spirit of Roman Catholicism, each figure—the star, the wheel, the double chain—has a religious significance. The "SS" of the double chain, for example, represents the *Santissimo Sacramento*, most holy sacrament.

33

A Madrileno instructs his curious son in the fine points of playing the zambomba.

With the sharp staccato roll of castanets echoing across the cavernous cathedral, the boys sing and whirl through a triumphant conclusion. They kneel and bow to the altar, and the dance is over.

The songs and dances of a Spanish Christmas generally are performed to the accompaniment of one or more traditional folk instruments. More elaborate instrumentation may also be employed, as in the Dance of the Sixes or the impressive midnight masses in the larger cathedrals. But even then, the booming sound of the organ or the woodwinds and brass of a full orchestra will be punctuated with the wooden clack of castanets or the strum of one or more guitars.

Two of the easiest—and, therefore, the most common—folk instruments to play are the tambourine and the *sonaja*. The latter is a round percussion instrument similar to the tambourine and made of rows of wire or thin strips of tin. These are strung with pairs of small tin disks.

The *zambomba* is another instrument that frequently accompanies the songs of carolers. It consists of a cylinder, approximately 10 inches high, with a skin stretched taut across the top to form a sort of drum. A lightweight stick is inserted through the bottom of the cylinder and pushed through a hole in the skin. The top of the stick projects upward and is often decorated with ribbons or colored paper flowers.

The zambomba may look like a drum, but it is not played like a drum or any other instrument. Instead of beating on the drumlike head, the player spits on his hand and moves the oiled stick up and down, producing a steady, rhythmic wail.

In northwest Spain the bagpipe is as purely Spanish as castanets are in the south. The people of Asturias and Galicia trace their heritage back to the Celts, a heritage that is still strongly apparent in the music, dances, and folklore of the region. Because the mountain ranges and heavy rains in northwestern Spain prevented the Moors from ever gaining a foothold there, the Galicians and Asturians still think of themselves as "pure" Spaniards. To the rest of the world, however, their Celtic temperament, a kind of lyrical, nostalgic melancholy that is called *saudade*, makes them as different from their fellow Spaniards as winter is from summer.

Many traditional northwestern dances, from the *vaqueira*, a kind of formal herders' dance, to the freewheeling *pericote*, are performed to the drone of the bagpipe. These dances contrast sharply to the more familiar flamenco of Andalusia.

No Andalusian Christmas would be complete without the fierce stamping of feet and rattling of castanets that characterize the flamenco—a fiery, passionate dance, strongly suggestive of Moorish influence. The emotional *cante jondo* often begins with a long, drawn-out, ear-piercing cry, like that of the Moslem *muezzin* calling the faithful to prayer from atop a high minaret. The music is usually performed on a guitar; the underlying gypsy beat is emphasized by the rhythmic clapping of hands.

The gay, yet understated, Catalan *sardana* could hardly be more different from the sensual flamenco. Pipes, flutes, oboes, or other woodwinds, rather than the guitar, usually accompany this dance. While the flamenco is danced singly or by couples, the sardana is performed by large groups, often arranged in concentric circles. Believed to be of Greek origin, the dance looks remarkably like a Greek folk dance—a happy, floating circle of dancers, moving and turning as one. Compared with the fiery flamenco, the sardana seems almost emotionless, yet graceful and effortless.

The sardana *plays such a popular role in Catalan culture that Barcelona has erected a monument to the dance.*

Despite its appearance, the sardana is a decidedly intricate dance, with a fixed number of steps to every bar of music. The dancers join hands in a circle, but after a certain number of bars, the hands change position. Individual dancers stay in one place for the greater part of the dance, carrying out an intricate toe-and-heel step. Then suddenly, as the music grows louder, the rings of dancers begin to spin, often in opposite directions. It is said that no one but a Catalan can dance the sardana without counting aloud.

At noon every summer Sunday the sardana is danced before the cathedral at Barcelona. It is also performed in the streets of every Catalan town and village during the Christmas holidays, to the tune of the beloved Catalan songs of joy—the *goigs*.

The "Carol of the Birds," popularized by Pablo Casals, is probably the most famous Catalan goig. But it is only one of hundreds that have sprung from the fertile poetic imagination of the region. These simple, happy tunes describe in delightful detail Biblical or imagined incidents surrounding the birth of the Christ Child. One of the most charming features a little shepherd boy who asks, "What Shall We Give to the Babe in the Manger?"

The song goes on to list most of the products that the region is known for, from raisins to figs, olives and nuts, cream cheese, honey, and lastly—why, a goig, of course!

The visit of the shepherds to the manger is one of the favorite subjects of the Spanish villancicos, but lullabies are also very popular. The poetic form of these traditional carols has a history that reaches back to the fourteenth century. A refrain begins and ends each song, with verses sung in between. The freedom of improvisation within the rigid structure dictated by tradition is truly extraordinary, but no more so than the amazing variety of song and dance that characterizes the Spanish Christmas.

Waiting for the Three Kings

Detail of an eighteenth-century nacimiento *showing*
Balthasar traveling to the Christ child.

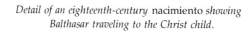

The passing of Christmas ushers in another phase of the holiday season—the long wait for the arrival of the Three Kings. These traditional gift bearers of the Spanish Christmas season do not distribute their presents until January 6, also known as the Feast of the Epiphany. The interval between December 25 and the Feast of the Epiphany constitutes the Twelve Days of Christmas—a period decidedly more secular in tone than the week or two before Christmas. Families spend a good deal of time window shopping and browsing through stores, so that the children can decide what they would like to ask the Kings to bring.

Dolls, stuffed animals, toy cars and trucks—these perennial favorites retain their classic appeal. But in the larger cities, at least, they compete for children's attention with the latest electronic games from the United States and Japan and a selection of other modern-day attractions equal to anything found around the world.

There may be a good deal of agonizing over choices before youngsters decide what to request for themselves and for other members of the family. The children wait until the last possible moment before composing a letter to the Kings containing their requests. The letters are drafted with painstaking care. Sentences are phrased and rephrased, spellings checked and corrected, and the final version may be recopied two or three times before it is at last judged satisfactory.

Urban children who wish to avoid these literary agonies may decide to deliver their requests orally. Many department stores hire people on a temporary basis to dress as the Three Kings and listen patiently to the children's wishes. Youngsters who are especially eager for the Kings' attention often stand in line for quite some time and then, as an extra reminder, hand over their letters at the end of the interview.

To avoid the accusation that they are selfish, Spanish youngsters always ask for things for other members of the family as well as for themselves. Parents admonish their children that if they do not behave, the Kings may leave them nothing but a lump of coal. Rarely, if ever, does a real lump of coal actually materialize on Three Kings' morning. But Spanish sweet shops display lumps of sugar colored black and shaped like coal as a means to keep mischievous little ones in line.

The Three Kings have long held a special place in the Spanish Christmas season. The oldest Spanish drama in existence, *Auto de los Reyes Magos,* tells the story of the Kings' search for the Christ child. It is the only example of Spanish liturgical drama that remains in existence today. Unfortunately only a fragment of about 150 lines has been preserved. No exact date is known for the fragment, but informed authorities place its composition at about 1150. The play was presented in the cathedral of Toledo, doubtless over many Christmases, with no costumes or stage settings except a star. Choirboys played all the roles.

The Three Kings appear onstage, first separately and then together, to discuss the mysterious new star in the east and what it might mean. Speaking in rhymed couplets, they decide the star must symbolize the birth of a messiah, and they resolve to visit the child and see which of their gifts he will choose—gold, frankincense, or myrrh. The scene shifts abruptly to Herod's palace, and the

An eager youngster carefully pens her Christmas wish list for consideration by the Three Kings.

Posting a letter to the Three Kings is no small task for these youngsters.

fragment breaks off as a worried Herod consults his astrologers to find out what the new star might augur.

The action of the play is simple and naive, which is not surprising, considering that this is one of the first plays written in a popular tongue, rather than in Latin. Still, the characterizations are realistic. The Kings are hesitant at first to follow the star, and Herod is quite believable as he broods over his astrologers' refusal to give him a definitive answer. It is easy to see in the fragment both the playwright's attempt to extract real drama from the story and the origins of the Three Kings' appeal to the Spanish imagination.

Most people are familiar with the rest of the story: the royal trio's arrival at last in Bethlehem; Herod's decision to eliminate the threat of future trouble by sending his soldiers to slay every newborn Jewish boy. Herod's grisly decision is commemorated today by the Roman Catholic Church at the Feast of the Holy Innocents, and December 28 is set aside as a day to honor Herod's victims.

The Feast of the Holy Innocents is still celebrated, and with great relish, by the people of Spain. But over the centuries, the natural mirth and spontaneity of children has transformed the occasion from a day of mourning to one of gaiety, gaming, and the playing of practical jokes. December 28 is today the Spanish equivalent of the American April Fool's Day.

Village lads in the Pyrenees build bonfires at the town gateways and from among their number elect a mock mayor, a sort of Spanish Lord of Misrule. This merry official is empowered to assess fines for alleged offenses, and he imposes an absurd law and order by forcing citizens to sweep the streets. Money from the fines is used to pay for a party.

Spanish youngsters, like those the world over, love to play games. Variations on "hide-and-seek" and "musical chairs," tag games and guessing games, "find the hidden object" games—all these and more are enjoyed during the post-Christmas holidays. Charades are especially popular, and Biblical stories in prose and verse are acted out with abandon.

On Holy Innocents Day, party-going youngsters divide themselves into two groups: soldiers and *los inocentes*. Soldiers write out verses or riddles and pin them to the backs of los inocentes. The latter have to figure out the contents by asking a series of yes-or-no questions.

Pum-puñete is another highly popular game. *Pum* is a Spanish expression meaning bang—an exclamation expressing a noise, explosion, or knock. Pum-puñete is simply a nonsense word. Spanish children, like children the world over, love to play with words: *arra, arra, la guitarra; ota, ota, la pelota*—nonsense rhymes on the words guitar (*guitarra*) and ball (*pelota*).

To play *pum-puñete*, youngsters stack up their closed fists in a high column. One of them begins to count, from the bottom up, touching each fist as he says a nonsense verse:

> *¿Cómo se llama este?* (What's the name of this one?)
> *–Pum-puñete.*
> *¿Y este?* (And this one?)
> *–Cascabelete.* (A nonsense word for jingle bells)

When the counter lands on a fist at the end of a verse, the player whose hand is in the column must reply instantly. If a youngster speaks out of turn, that is, when his fist has not been touched, he has to pay a forfeit.

When the versifier reaches the top of the column, all the players inflate their cheeks. With fists still clenched, they go about trying to deflate their friends' puffy cheeks. The first person to laugh pays a forfeit, and the last player with inflated cheeks wins a prize.

The next high point in the long wait for the Three Kings is, of course, New Year's Eve. Spaniards ring out the old year and welcome the new with a great deal of gaiety and laughter, much like the rest of the world. But in the countryside especially, this universal holiday is observed with a few uniquely Spanish customs.

Throughout the country friends and neighbors spend the evening feasting and making merry. Bands of young people patrol the streets, often clad in costumes and disguised by masks. They celebrate the arrival of the new year with singing and dancing, accompanied, as usual, by the strange wail of zambombas and the merry jingling of castanets.

Children who want to make their wishes known in person go to visit the Three Kings at a local department store.

A candy store owner arranges a tempting display of
dulces *to attract window shoppers.*

The wealthier Spanish families celebrate the occasion in truly elaborate fashion. At their banquets, every conceivable delicacy is temptingly displayed. Gentlemen wear white tie and tails, and the ladies don their most elegant gowns, accented by precious jewels and the finest lace.

Residents of the larger cities select whatever entertainment suits their fancy and their pocketbooks. Luxury hotels and restaurants offer entertainment packages that combine dinner and dancing. Opera and theater buffs have a variety of performances from which to choose. Music lovers may go to hear a classical recital or test the limits of their endurance at an ear-splitting rock concert.

In smoky *tavernas,* dancers perform the amazing variety of folk dances to which Spain has given birth: the butterfly-like *bolero;* the *giraldilla* of Seville; the fandango of Huelva; or the *jota* of Aragon. And, of course, in almost every music hall or nightclub, a gypsy woman in mantilla, high comb, sleeveless bodice, and wide, flounced skirts stamps and claps her way through the extraordinary flamenco.

The end of the old year and birth of the new offers yet another excuse for enjoying a hearty and elaborate dinner. In all but the poorest homes, the New Year's Eve meal is washed down with generous glasses of champagne and topped off with the traditional holiday dessert, turrón.

Pork is a popular favorite as a New Year's Eve entree. Perhaps this tradition goes back to the ancient custom of sacrificing a wild boar in honor of the new year. The *cochinillo* (suckling pig) served in Segovia, north of Madrid, is especially succulent. Since Spain has a dearth of both grazing

land and cooking fuel, the Iberians long ago adopted the practice of raising small animals and slaughtering them young. The delicate flavor and crispness of the Segovian cochinillo provide a memorable culinary experience.

In Andalusia, the provincial capital of Granada produces an extraordinary, pungent, dark-red ham, which is offered as an appetizer in thin, almost translucent slices. *Jamón serrano* is sun-cured on the heights of the Sierra Nevadas, which loom to the south of the city.

There is a widespread belief in Spain that the pig brings good luck for the new year. It has been said that this belief arose because the pig roots in a forward direction—supposedly indicative of a "fat future." People who eat turkey, goose, or other fowl on New Year's Eve are asking for bad luck in the coming year, as fowl scratch backward when searching for food.

Throughout Spain, it is a New Year's tradition, as the clock strikes midnight, to pop a grape or raisin into one's mouth with each chime of the clock. This is to insure that the twelve months of the coming year will be happy ones.

The place to be in Madrid as midnight approaches on December 31 is the Puerta del Sol (Gate of the Sun), the major crossroads of the city and, in fact, of all Spain. The square serves as the "zero point" for measuring distances to other parts of the country.

It is also the place where the clock that sets the time standard for all of Spain is located. Atop the Ministerio de la Gobernación building, a golden ball descends at midnight to mark the passing of the old year. Spaniards flock to the square by the thousands to mark the event. Television crews provide live coverage of the crowd, so that those watching at home can eat their grapes in "official" time in front of their TV sets.

The Puerta del Sol has a long and fascinating history and has been the scene of many stirring events. The most famous is probably the uprising against the French that occurred there in 1808, memorialized in Goya's famous painting, *The 3rd of May 1808: The Execution of the Defenders of Madrid.*

For many Spaniards, the New Year's festivities continue throughout the night. Teen-agers and adults alike wend their way from one noisy party to another. At every house they are greeted with showers of streamers and sent on their way in a hail of confetti. The laughter and merriment continue until dawn.

Around five or six in the morning, the typical group of partygoers will head for a café or bar for thick, foamy hot chocolate and *churros,* the Spanish equivalent of doughnuts. Churros are made by piping long, thick ropes of dough from a sort of pastry gun into a cauldron of boiling oil. The dough fries up crisp and brown and is sold in semicircles about 6 inches long.

The combination of hot chocolate and churros is a popular year-round breakfast in many parts of Spain. Churros are seldom made at home, however; the high cost of cooking fuel makes it im-

"Lucky" toy pigs have a party in this New Year's Eve window display.

practical to fry up just a few churros in the family kitchen. Most Spaniards either obtain them from a street vendor for a few pesetas, or go to a bar or café.

For the same reason, few homemakers in central and southern Spain make their own bread. The donkey cart from the local *panadería* makes daily deliveries of crusty, round loaves every morning. Later in the day, children may be sent to the bakery for another loaf or two for dinner—Spanish people do not like to eat "stale" bread.

One of the best known of the old *churrerías*, or pastry or doughnut shops, in Madrid is behind the Church of San Ginés, more or less around the corner from the Puerta del Sol. In the days when the Puerta del Sol was famous for its bustling, all-night cafés, the San Ginés churreria often served as the last stop for merrymakers who had passed the night in drinking and socializing.

It is not at all unusual to see people in evening clothes at the churrerias early on New Year's morning. Nor is it uncommon to see jewel-laden ladies in floor-length gowns escorted to early morning mass on January 1 by gentlemen in tuxedos. Having welcomed the new year in with revelry, then reverence, most Spaniards spend the rest of the day recovering.

Far to the north of windswept Madrid, in the shadow of the high Pyrenees, ancient customs live on among the fiercely independent Basques and Catalans. On the last night of the old year, fairies, or *hados*, are supposed to come, bringing good luck in the right hand and bad luck in the left.

Pyreneans open doors to the fairies and even give them their own special room, spotlessly clean and supplied with a meal of bread and wine. The church fathers banned this custom more than fifteen hundred years ago, but the prohibition seems to have had little effect.

In the morning, the master of the house checks the fairies' room. If there is any bread left over, he breaks it up and distributes it among all the members of the household. It is said that villagers who provide liberally for the hados are rewarded in the new year with large harvests and increased flocks.

This custom seems related to the Bacchanalia of ancient Rome—the revels held in honor of the god of wine and merrymaking. The Romans believed that the dead returned to their homes for these riotous celebrations and were therefore careful to prepare for the return of the departed. The Romans spread tables for the family ghosts and even went so far as to leave dice out so that the ghosts could have something to amuse themselves with while the living feasted and danced.

In parts of the Pyrenees, the first day of the new year is celebrated with carnivals. This is yet another custom that the church tried to put an end to long ago, but with no more success than efforts to stop the un-Christian practice of leaving out food for the fairies.

It is not difficult to understand why the Pyrenean New Year's carnivals provoked clerical disapproval. The participants' behavior can be, at times, rather ribald. There is singing and dancing in the streets, of course. But besides the traditional villancicos and goigs, the repertoire in certain areas includes many bawdy tunes and ditties.

Mumming and mummers' plays are another common element of the carnivals. This form of holiday merrymaking dates back to the Roman Saturnalia—the week-long, mid-December feast held in honor of the god of agriculture, Saturn. In Roman times throngs of celebrants crowded the streets, dressed in every conceivable costume. Men donned women's clothes, and masks shaped like animals' heads were especially popular.

By medieval times the custom was widespread and practiced enthusiastically throughout much of

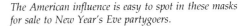

The American influence is easy to spot in these masks for sale to New Year's Eve partygoers.

For good luck, many Spaniards eat one grape for each stroke of the clock at midnight on New Year's Eve.

southern and eastern Europe. Both church and state disapproved of it. Mumming seemed to lend itself to wild behavior, and disguises and masks made it all but impossible to identify criminals who took advantage of the general confusion to rob, steal, and even murder. But mumming proved as difficult to suppress as other folk customs that stem from ancient times.

The Pyrenean mummers' plays that survive today in the new year's carnivals often feature one or more characters dressed as bears. The appearance of the bear, a creature that still roams wild in parts of the Pyrenees, is the signal for general abandon.

In the valley of the Baztan, a character called Olentzero sits in the corner of the village tavern on New Year's Eve, with a cauldron on his head and a scythe in his hand. After Olentzero has been properly chastised, the village lads take him outside and carry him from house to house, singing as they go. The wassailing, or toasting, of fruit trees to ensure a good harvest is another New Year's task performed by village boys in this region of Spain.

Trials of strength are a popular way to celebrate the new year in Basque country. The blood-curdling noises made by the participants as they test each other's powers are startling evidence of this proud people's close ties to an older, more primitive culture. In certain remote valleys, entire villages pit themselves against each other, the attackers announcing their approach with ringing bells and waving sticks.

In the northwest, the New Year's custom of electing a King of the Wren has close parallels with a practice followed in certain parts of Britain and Ireland. The parallels are not surprising, considering the Celtic heritage of the region.

For centuries on the Isle of Man, in the Irish Sea between England and Ireland, people would gather after midnight mass to hunt and kill a wren. The hapless bird was fastened to a pole and taken from house to house at daybreak. Parishioners collected all the money they could, then went to the churchyard in solemn procession and buried the wren. Only then could Christmas begin officially.

The custom may have had its roots in pre-Christian animal sacrifices, which in turn may have substituted for human sacrifices. At any rate, the practice has been modified considerably in modern Ireland. A bunch of feathers has replaced the wren, and the custom is used merely to raise money for a holiday dance for young people.

*Crowds gather outside Barcelona's City Hall to ring
out the old year and welcome the new.*

Bells over Bethlehem
(Campana Sobre Campana)

Traditional Andalucian [GKE]

Traditional Andalucian Carol [WE]

Allegro

1.¡Cam-pa-na so-bre cam-pa - na   Cam-pa-na so-bre cam-pa - na!
1.Bells o-ver Beth-le-hem peal - ing,   God's sa-cred pres-ence re-veal - ing!

A - só-ma-te a la ven-ta - na   Ve-ras a un Ni-ño en la cu - na.
There in a cra-dle is rest - ing   Je - sus, the earth's rich-est bless - ing!

REFRAIN

"Be - lén, cam-pa-nas de Be - lén, Qué los an-ge-les to-can Que nue-vas me tra-óis?"
The bells, the bells of Beth-le - hem Are ring-ing out the ti-dings, "good will __ to all men!"

Re - co-gi - do tu re-ba-no A dón-de vas pas-tor-ci-to __
Leave your sheep __ and come, O shep-herds, pres-ents bring the Babe so low - ly, __

Voy a lle-var al por-tal __ Re - que-són, man te-ca y vi - no." Be-
Bring some cheese and bring some wine __ For the Moth - er Ma - ry ho - ly. The

lén, cam-pa-nas de Be - lén, Qué los an-ge-les to-can, Qué nue-vas me tra-ois?"
bells, the bells of Beth-le - hem Are ring-ing out the ti-dings, "Good will __ to all men!"

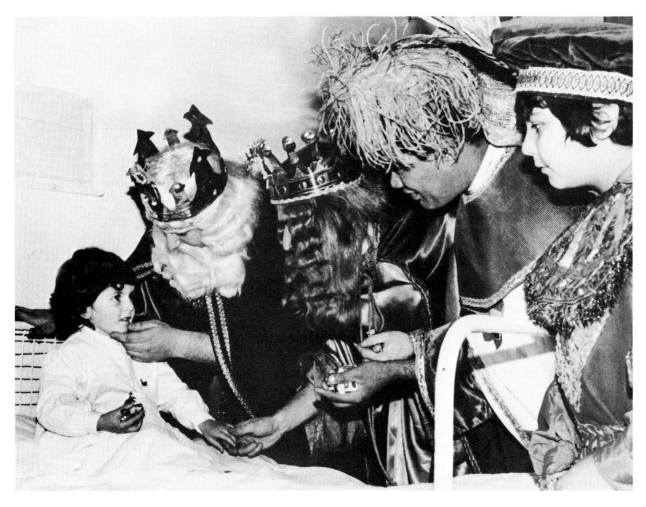

The Three Kings and a page boy pay a call on a hospitalized child. No one is forgotten as the great day approaches.

Not so in the mountains of northwest Spain, however. The men of the village choose a leader, who in turn assembles a hunting party and heads out into the surrounding countryside. Armed with sticks, they kill a wren and return triumphantly to the village. The bird is fixed to a long pole and garlanded with olive and oak leaves and mistletoe. King and victim are paraded through the streets with a great deal of fanfare on Three Kings' Day, thus bringing the Christmas holidays to an official, if somewhat gruesome, conclusion.

The days between Christmas and January 6 are a delightful, fascinating blend of Christian beliefs and secular customs in Spain. Even Santa Claus may have made a brief Christmas Day or Christmas Eve appearance at the homes of some of the more widely traveled urban families. But his hold on the hearts and minds of Spanish youngsters hardly equals that of the beloved royal figures from the east. As January 6 approaches, the children's excitement rises to a fever pitch.

The Three Kings Arrive

*This elaborate Epiphany scene decorates the major
altar at the Cathedral of Toledo.*

Spanish tradition holds that the Three Kings (or Magi) from the East set out for Spain each year on January 5, the eve of the Epiphany, to pay homage to the infant Christ. They don their finest robes, mount their horses, camels, or donkeys, and leave with an elaborate retinue of pack animals and servants.

In the past it was customary to go out to meet the Magi on Three Kings' Eve. Young and old alike would march to the edge of town or to the city gates carrying cakes for the Kings, plus a selection of straw, carrots, oats, and assorted other foods for the Kings' animals and servants.

The children trudged along with lamps mounted on poles and torches held aloft so that the Three Kings could find their way more easily. There was, of course, a certain amount of self-interest in this act of kindness. It was well known that the Kings were bearing gifts, not only for the Holy Infant, but for every child in Spain.

Parents in the procession carried rattles and bells along to provide a warm-hearted welcome for the great caravan. They blew horns and beat on pots and pans with spoons and sticks. Someone in the group usually brought along a ladder. Every once in a while the lookout would stop, set up his ladder, and peer into the night to see if he could locate *los reyes magos*.

These elaborate and well-intentioned efforts, however, never seemed to succeed. No matter how sharp the lookout, the Kings always seemed to pass by the town on another road. One would think they would have seen the lights or heard the noise made by the welcoming committee. But somehow the two groups always seemed to miss each other.

There was nothing for the youngsters to do but throw away the straw, eat the cakes and goodies themselves, and return home, weary and disappointed. But then the parents would suggest that the Three Kings had probably assembled at the great nacimiento in the village church. It sometimes took some talking to persuade sleepy little ones to check at the church before going to bed. But as is usually the case, the parents won out.

In the radiant candlelight illuminating the communal nacimiento, the villagers would discover Melchior, Gaspar, and Balthazar kneeling reverently before the Christ child, presenting their gifts of gold, frankincense, and myrrh. The entire community would join in singing the traditional Epiphany carol, "This Morn I Met the Train of the Kings." (Strictly speaking, of course, this claim was not accurate.)

It appears that the Spanish church played a significant role in assigning to the Feast of the Epiphany the prominence it now enjoys. In fourth-century Spain, a long fast marked the season of Advent, which in those times ended January 6. A document from the council of Saragossa, which dates from around 380, decreed a 21-day fast, from December 17 to January 6. During this time, the faithful were not supposed to dance or make merry, but were instead to devote themselves to prayer and worship. Certain prelates even refused to perform the marriage rites during this period. Needless to say, the feast that marked the end of Advent was celebrated with gusto.

The word *epiphany* comes from a Greek word meaning "manifestation" or "revelation." In an-

On Three Kings' Eve, Spanish children put out straw, food, and water for the royal animals and leave their shoes to be filled by the Kings themselves.

cient times the Feast of the Epiphany commemorated Christ's nativity, which was assumed to have taken place on January 6. The day was also associated with the baptism of Jesus, an event that marked the beginning of Christ's ministry on earth and revealed him to be the Son of God. This was thought to have occurred on his thirtieth birthday.

After December 25 was widely accepted as Christ's actual birthday, the Feast of the Epiphany became associated with the arrival of the Magi in Bethlehem, since they were the first to whom the Messiah was revealed through the miraculous appearance of the Christmas star. To this day January 6, Three Kings' Day, is also known as "little Christmas" or "old Christmas" in certain parts of Spain.

Spaniards still go out to meet the Three Kings on the evening of January 5. But in larger towns and cities, at least, their efforts are rewarded by a *cabalgata*, a festive and showy parade that brings the Kings to town in grand fashion.

At no time during the Christmas holidays is the Spanish love of color and pageantry more readily apparent than on Epiphany Eve. Youngsters and their parents alike line the streets to welcome the royal visitors and their entourage. The stars of the cabalgata appear in full regalia. Crowned heads glisten and gleam with artificial gems. The Kings' long, trailing robes, adorned with fanciful embroidery, amaze and delight the onlookers.

The Magi may sweep past on flower-bedecked floats, waving to their admirers and tossing candy and little treats to wide-eyed youngsters. Balthazar is the children's favorite; it is he who most commonly distributes turrón and other goodies.

Sometimes the Kings are perched atop live animals. Balthazar usually rides a donkey. The other Kings may be mounted on horseback or, in the bigger parades, they may even sway through town aboard camels.

It would be most unseemly for the Kings to travel alone. The fancier and more elaborate their entourage, the better, from satin-clad pages and court jesters to every imaginable kind of servant. Marching bands may precede the royal trio, clearing a path and, with their booming bass drums, setting the pace for the cabalgata. Jugglers, clowns, stilt-walkers, and mummers in fanciful costumes also join in the festivities.

Cabalgatas are held in most of the larger towns and cities on the evening of January 5. The larger the community, the bigger and more colorful the parade. Madrid, Barcelona, Palma de Mallorca, Santillana del Mar, Lerida, and Villafranca del Panadés put on wonder-filled, elaborate cabalgatas.

Holiday excitement seems to reach a peak on the eve of Three Kings' Day. Many stores stay open until midnight to accommodate last-minute shoppers. There is probably no other night in the year on which Spanish parents have a more difficult time persuading their children to go to bed—or on which children find it harder to drift off to sleep.

Just before retiring, every member of the family puts out a pair of shoes, with full confidence that during the night the Kings will come to fill the shoes with presents and treats. Children, parents, and grandparents alike participate in this tradition. In the long rows of apartment buildings and condominium complexes that provide housing for the majority of urban Spaniards, shoes are placed outside on the balconies. They may also be put at the window, the door, or near the fireplace.

In most families, parents will leave out three dishes of food for the Kings, and perhaps three glasses of wine as well. The animals are not forgotten, either. The children usually stuff their shoes with straw for the royal camels, or they will leave out oats, barley, carrots or other delicacies, depending on the kind of transportation they imagine the gift bringers are riding.

Some families possess two different sets of Kings for the family nacimiento. One set shows the trio astride camels. It is put in place on Christmas Eve and left there until January 5, to show that the Kings are en route to Bethlehem. On the Eve of the Epiphany, a new set of Kings replaces the first after the children have gone to sleep. This one shows the trio kneeling devotedly before the crib, presenting their gifts—proof that the Kings have arrived at the manger and have visited the household during the night. In homes with only one set of Kings, parents simply move the figures closer to the crib on the night of January 5.

The children can barely contain their excitement the morning of January 6. They get up at the crack of dawn to inspect their shoes and see what the Kings have brought for them. The straw, of course, has disappeared, as has the food left out for the Magi. The children's shoes are stuffed with candy and other treats and surrounded with presents. So, in fact, are the shoes put out by the grown-up members of the family.

In many parts of Spain, wealthy members of the community will visit the homes of the poor on the night of January 5. They empty shoes of straw and replace it with fruit, nuts, turrón, and other sweetmeats.

Melchior, Gaspar, and Balthazar extend a royal
greeting to the good citizens of Barcelona.

Joyful crowds line the route of the cabalgata, *or parade of the Three Kings.*

King Melchior, attended by a page boy, meets a few of his younger subjects at the Barcelona cabalgata.

A Spanish Christmas Vocabulary

Belenista: A club or organization devoted to building and admiring nativity or Bethlehem scenes, organizing displays, and sponsoring competitions.

Besugo: Baked sea bream, the traditional fish course of the Spanish Christmas meal.

Cabalgata: The parade held in the larger towns and cities on January 5 to welcome the Three Kings.

El Natal: Christmas.

Felices Pascuas de Navidad: Merry Christmas (literally, "Happy Holiday of the Nativity").

Goigs: Catalonian songs of joy.

Los Inocentes: The Jewish male babies slaughtered by Herod's soldiers, commemorated by a feast on December 28.

Los Reyes Magos: The Three Kings.

Los Seises: The Dance of the Sixes; performed by choirboys in traditional costume before the altar of the Seville Cathedral on December 8 to usher in the holidays.

Mazapán: Marzipan, a candy widely eaten at Christmastime.

Misa del Gallo: Christmas Eve midnight mass (literally, "mass of the cock's crow").

Nacimiento: The crèche or nativity scene that is found in almost every Spanish home at Christmastime.

Noche buena: Christmas Eve (literally, the "good night").

Pavo: Turkey, the main course of the traditional Spanish Christmas meal.

Paz en la Tierra a los Hombres de Buena Voluntad: Peace on Earth to People of Good Will.

Próspero año nuevo: Happy New Year.

Roscón: The traditional treat for Three Kings' Day, a fruitcake with an inexpensive toy hidden inside.

Tío: Yule log.

Tuna: A lively band of university students in traditional costume who sing and play music.

Turrón: A kind of nougat made of toasted almonds, sugar, honey, and eggs, eaten universally during the Christmas holidays.

Villancicos: Traditional Spanish Christmas carols.

Zambomba: A hollow, cylindrical folk instrument that produces a rhythmic whine when a stick is moved up and down through a skin stretched over the top; widely used to accompany Christmas carols.

The Three Kings are strangely appealing to the Spanish imagination and, in fact, to Christendom at large. The role they play in the celebration of Christmas is especially remarkable when one considers that the only real mention of these characters is a brief account in the Gospel of St. Matthew. It does not supply their names, tell us where they came from, or, for that matter, even specify how many they were.

Over the years after Matthew penned his account, the Magi began to take on a life of their own. Each acquired a name, a background, a unique personality. Eventually, they were even given their own feast day.

There is a certain magic and mysterious appeal in Matthew's account of the Magi. They were apparently the only ones to whom the Christmas star appeared. It guided them safely to the manger in Bethlehem, and divine intervention kept the Kings from revealing Christ's birthplace to the wicked Herod.

Clearly, people wanted to believe in the story of the Three Kings. Their presence at the manger adds a symbolic touch to the scene. At one end of the scale, humble shepherds (mentioned in St. Luke's Nativity account) kneel in adoration of the newborn Savior. At the other end, the royal visitors submit their temporal power to the divine authority of the Christ child.

At first the Three Kings were not kings at all. The Latin word *magi* in the early scriptures refers

Roscón, the traditional treat for Three Kings' Day, contains a hidden good luck charm.

specifically to Persian astrologer-priests. As time went on, embellishers added the meaning of wise men/philosophers. It was not until the end of the sixth century that magi and "kings" were used interchangeably to refer to Matthew's star-guided visitors. This was due to the work of the scholar Tertullian, who linked the travelers to two Old Testament prophecies that kings bearing gifts would come to Israel.

The popular imagination was stirred as much by the nature of the regal gifts as it was by speculation on the identity of the bearers. Gold, of course, is a precious metal; frankincense and myrrh, aromatic resins, were highly valued as incense. Later the gifts acquired symbolic meaning as well. Gold was understood to stand for the virtue of love and also to symbolize Christ as the king of the world. Frankincense, a very sweet spice, became identified with prayer or with Christ as the king of heaven. Myrrh, which comes from the bark of a thorny African tree, came to represent suffering and the sacrifice that Christ made on the cross.

One church scholar, Jacobus de Voragine, had a more practical interpretation of the Magi's gifts: the gold was intended to relieve the Holy Family's poverty; frankincense would be useful in disguising objectionable stable smells; and myrrh could be used as an antidote for vermin.

Matthew's mention of three gifts was ultimately responsible for a papal decree that the Magi were three in number. Early church art portrays two or four gift bearers. St. Augustine preferred the number 12, symbolic of the 12 apostles and the 12 tribes of Israel.

By the eighth century, the oldest of the three Magi was called Melchior. Gaspar was a young man, and Balthazar was often pictured as a black man, one who had traveled from faraway Ethiopia.

At some point in the growth of the Three Kings legend, the figures passed into Spanish folklore and became responsible for distributing gifts to worthy children. In other countries this task fell to Santa Claus, St. Nicholas, Befana (in Italy), or even the Christ child himself. But in Spain it is the Kings who are the source of youngster's delight at Christmastime.

Spanish presents are not exchanged from one person to another. The Kings give them all. On January 6, once the children have opened their gifts at home, the family most likely will go to visit relatives to see what the Kings may have left for them there. Visitors also will bring along gifts that the Kings have left at their house for cousins, aunts, uncles, and other members of the extended family.

The traditional Kings' Day treat is *roscón,* a kind of fruitcake with a tiny, inexpensive toy hidden inside. Roscón is delicious and much loved. It is served either plain or topped with luscious whipped cream. On Three Kings' Day, Spaniards will eat as much roscón as possible, and as often as possible: at breakfast, lunch, and in the afternoon as a snack.

Anyone who discovers the toy in his or her piece of roscón is destined to enjoy good luck in the coming year. Should a parent be served the trinket, the mother or father will most likely "cheat" and sneak it back into a piece of roscón that is destined for one of the children. Little ones get a huge amount of pleasure from guessing who will find the toy, but especially from discovering it themselves.

Three Kings' Day brings the Spanish Christmas holidays to a happy conclusion. The lilting strains of the traditional villancicos seem to fade with the last rays of the sun, not to be heard again for another year. The family nacimiento is packed away

Spanish children and grownups alike get up early on Three Kings' morning to see what the visitors have brought.

lovingly with the other holiday decorations. Families who put up Christmas trees know that the time has come to take them down. Children who had so much trouble getting to sleep the night before go to bed willingly on Three Kings' Day. The excitement is over at last, and they have much to dream about.

The Christmas Story in Art

This Catalan Nativity scene is on display at the
Museum of Decorative Arts in Madrid.

Through the centuries, Spanish artists have portrayed the Christmas story in paintings, frescoes, sculptures, wood carvings, and many other mediums. Their exquisite works decorate huge cathedrals, humble monasteries, and grand museums throughout the country.

No aspect of the Christmas story has escaped the attention of Spanish artists—from the angel Gabriel's surprise visit announcing to Mary that she is to become the mother of God to the Holy Family's flight into Egypt to protect their newborn son from Herod's legions.

Outstanding portrayals of the Nativity by traditional artists include works by El Greco, Velázquez, and the sculptures of the Transparente in the Toledo Cathedral. Barcelona's Sagrada Familia, the church designed by Antonio Gaudí, is a modern, and quite controversial, tribute to the Holy Family.

On a different, but no less important, scale, the story of the Nativity has fired the imaginations of generations of Spanish folk artists. The creation of nacimiento scenes for family, village, school, and church has been a universal pre-Christmas activity in Spain for centuries, and it is only natural that this popular folk art has reached a high level of development.

Spanish nacimiento figures have been fashioned from every conceivable material: wood, clay, wax, plaster, straw, even cardboard. Often there are several artisans involved in the creation of the elaborate nacimientos produced by the belenistas, the clubs and organizations devoted to building and displaying the crèches or Bethlehems. A skilled woodworker might transform a piece of scrap pine into a figure of Balthazar, the Ethiopian King. A local housepainter-turned-artisan might color in the hands and face of the Magi figure, then turn it over to a seamstress or tailor to be fitted for royal robes. Yet another set of skilled fingers might decorate the robes with rich embroidery, then send the king to a metalsmith or jeweler to be crowned.

So many outstanding nacimientos have been produced in Spain that a special museum has been created to collect and preserve them. Located in Murcia, it is 30 miles (48 kilometers) from Cartagena on the southeast coast. One crèche on display in the museum, created by the popular sculptor Francisco Salzillo (1707–1781), contains no less than 372 animals and 184 little figures of peasants. All carved from wood, they possess an amazing vitality.

Every Spanish town and village seems to have one or two families who are particularly adept at the creation of nacimiento figures. But the Salzillo family surely must hold the record for mass production. Francisco, together with his sister and brothers, is said to have produced a total of 4000

This is a single example of the more than 1500 nacimiento displays on exhibition in a special museum at Murcia.

Through the ages, few subjects have proved more compelling to Spanish artists than the madonna and child.

wooden figures in his lifetime.

The theme of the madonna and child has been interpreted by countless Spanish artists since the beginning of the Christian era. These polychrome wooden sculptures display two stern examples from the Romanesque period and a far more approachable representation dating from the Renaissance.

The top figure is from the early twelfth century. Few free-standing sculptures were created during this period. The Romanesque was essentially an architectural style, and most sculpture was executed in relief as simple adornment, subordinate to the building as a whole. This example is intended to be viewed, or worshiped, from the front only, the sides being originally hidden in an architectural niche.

Romanesque sculptors were preoccupied with evoking the spiritual quality of a subject, rather than capturing a three-dimensional representation. The artist has chosen to emphasize the madonna's eyes, considered to be windows to the soul. The statue is frozen in a timeless universe of the spirit, far removed from our own sensual world. The piece has a primitive vitality that is typically Catalan. The approach is direct, forceful, unpretentious, clearly the product of a folk artist. A strong Byzantine influence can also be seen in the exuberant use of color and very formal approach to the Christ child. He is not a newborn, but rather a miniature adult, regal in bearing, giving his blessing.

The middle statue is another example from the same period. It has that static, other-world quality characteristic of the Romanesque, but the emphasis is different. Here the madonna and child are monarchs, the king and queen of heaven. Both figures are crowned, and they are seated on a throne. This is a departure from the more provincial treatment of the Catalan mother and child. Still, the movement in the middle piece is away from the worldly. It is meant to excite our spiritual nature, to redirect our gaze toward heaven. The eyes are even more pronounced, and both figures seem frozen in eternity. The Byzantine influence is still strong, especially in the stripes decorating the throne.

Renaissance artists took a more humanistic approach in their work. The third example dates from the mid-1500s. The flat, two-dimensional quality of the Romanesque has been discarded. The piece is fluid, richly textured, and fully realistic. The Christ child is a rosy-cheeked baby, not a little adult. The madonna is warm, sweet, maternal—very human, definitely approachable. Except for the madonna's costume, this mother and child might be found in our own century.

Romanesque artists would never have dreamed of picturing Christ as a naked baby. But Renaissance artists characteristically celebrated the human body for itself. The emphasis here is on Christ's humanity. The way to salvation, by Renaissance times, lay in full participation in the life of this world, not in stony contemplation of the next.

The seventeenth century produced numerous artistic interpretations of the events of the Nativity, including masterworks by three of Spain's greatest artists: Juan Martínez Montañés, El Greco, and Diego Rodríguez de Silva y Velázquez.

Montañés is generally recognized as Spain's greatest sculptor in wood. Born in 1568, he passed the examinations for master sculptor at the age of 20. During his long life (he died in 1649), he produced a vast quantity of work, almost all devoted to religious subjects.

Christ on the Cross, commissioned in 1603 by the Archdeacon Vázquez de Leca, established Montañés's reputation as a sculptor. It is considered the most perfect Spanish example of this demanding subject. The happier theme of the Nativity is best represented by the artist's *Adoration of the Shepherds*.

Like most of Montañés's statues, the *Adoration* is gilded and painted in oil, probably by the artist's friend Francisco Pacheco. It measures 47 inches by 79 inches and is crafted with loving attention to detail. A curious ox and donkey, for example, poke their heads out from their stall to see what is disturbing the stable's customary quiet. Wisps of straw extend from the donkey's mouth, its pleasure in its evening snack forever captured in wood. Completed between 1610 and 1613, the *Adoration of the Shepherds* can be seen today at the Monastery of San Isidro del Campo in Santiponce.

Domenikos Theotokopoulos (1541?–1614), called El Greco by admirers in his adopted country, Spain, occupies a unique niche in the history of art. He was born in Crete and studied in Venice, but the Spaniards claimed him as their own. His work, however, transcends national borders and can only be described as distinctively his own.

El Greco had no contemporary biographers, and none of his diaries or theoretical writings has ever been found. In 1977, however, Dr. Fernando Marías of the Universidad Autónoma de Madrid and his colleague Dr. Agustín Bustamante discovered a sixteenth-century edition of Vitruvius' *On Architecture* that contained notes in El Greco's distinctive, Mediterranean mix of Italian, Spanish, and Greek. The artist wrote that the ladies of Toledo who wore high-heeled shoes (*chapines*) knew more about beauty than artists of the time who utilized mathematical formulas to meet Renaissance standards of perspective and proportion.

El Greco was familiar with the works of the Italian Renaissance, having lived in Italy for almost 20 years in the 1560s and 1570s. During his stay, he became familiar with the Venetian style of painting known as mannerism, which is marked by long, graceful lines, elongated and abstract forms, and metallic colors accented with white highlights. The influence of this approach to painting is readily apparent in his later work.

El Greco moved to Toledo, Spain, in 1577, and it was in Spain that he created his greatest paintings. Something in the country's religious atmosphere seems to have drawn forth and nourished his inborn mysticism. "The light of day clouds the inner light," he once told a friend who found him shut up in his studio, with shutters drawn, on a beautiful summer day.

If the search for inner light was the driving force of El Greco's personality, the bold, imaginative use of color and light also characterized his greatest paintings. Nowhere is this more apparent than in his magnificent *Adoration of the Shepherds*— the same subject that inspired the sculptor Montañés.

El Greco's painting is one of the most transcendent interpretations of the Nativity ever put to canvas. The Christ child at the heart of the picture is the primary source of light, radiating with an intensity that throws every other figure in the composition into sharp relief. The swirling ring of cherubs above, the elongated figures of the shepherds—all are transfigured by the Light of the World.

El Greco used to fashion small figures in wax, then arrange and rearrange them in groups, like a Spanish child playing with the family nacimiento. In the *Adoration of the Shepherds*, the composition perfectly expresses El Greco's transcendent theme. The worshipers are arranged in a lyrical upward spiral, with the Christ child at the center. The shepherd standing on the right seems about to be transported into heaven. The angels above are buoyed by the baby's spiritual energy.

The *Adoration* was the last painting El Greco produced. It was intended to hang above his tomb in the Church of Santo Domingo el Antiguo in Toledo, where he had painted his earliest works in Spain. In 1619, five years after El Greco's death, his son, Jorge Manuel Theotokopoulos, moved the family vault to San Torcuato in Toledo. The church was destroyed in the nineteenth century, and the artist's tomb vanished with it. Fortunately, the *Adoration of the Shepherds* still hangs today in the church of Toledo's cloistered Convent of Santo Domingo el Antiguo.

Velázquez's *Adoration of the Magi* is another

El Greco's Adoration of the Shepherds *(1614) was
created as a memorial to himself. It was the last
painting the artist produced, a magnificent conclusion
to his career.*

Velázquez's subdued approach to the Epiphany expressed the temperament of a successful court painter. The Adoration of the Magi *dates from 1619.*

Madrid's Museum of Decorative Arts contains many fine examples of Spanish nacimientos. This one is from the southeastern province of Murcia.

seventeenth-century work, painted approximately five years after El Greco completed the *Adoration of the Shepherds.* A comparison between the two is revealing.

Velázquez (1500–1660) was for most of his career a successful court painter, interested primarily in portraits and secular themes. So it is natural that when he turned to the Nativity, the subjects he chose were royal visitors, not humble shepherds. Velázquez, like El Greco, knew the importance of light and shadow. But in Velázquez's painting, the figures are thrown into relief by the last rays of a setting sun, not illuminated by the Christ child's inner light.

The *Adoration of the Magi* is a static composition, painted early in the artist's career (1619). Velázquez's wife and baby served as the models for madonna and child; he included his teacher, Pacheco, in the role of the grey-bearded king. The characters have their feet planted firmly on the ground. While the Magi exhibit reverent devotion, no one is about to rise into heaven. (El Greco's masterpiece, on the other hand, is transcendent and ecstatic—the conclusion of his life's work.)

The Transparente—an enormous baroque altarpiece in Toledo's Gothic cathedral—is unsurpassed in theatricality, even in a century of extraordinarily dramatic architecture. Created by Narcisco Tóme between 1721 and 1732, the work is an ornate confection of clouds, columns, saints, and angels in both low and high relief. In the central vaulted niche rests a skillfully mounted ma-

donna and child executed in marble, jasper, and bronze. The Transparente is illuminated by an aperture in the roof. The effect produced by the light falling upon the altarpiece is nothing short of breathtaking.

Barcelona's Templo Expiatorio de la Sagrada Familia is a modern-day, and controversial, tribute to the Holy Family. It has been variously described as "early psychedelic," "the most extravagant fancy ever conceived in ecclesiastical architecture," "glorious," "bizarre," "a work of genius," and "Gaudí's folly."

The building is the masterwork of Antonio Gaudí, whose death—he was run over by a tram in 1926—was as surrealistic as his distinctive architectural style. Begun in the 1880s, the Sagrada Familia has still not been completed.

The main porch is topped by a gigantic stone Christmas tree, painted a climactic green. Four enormously tall fluted pinnacles taper oddly to the sky, each capped by a sort of giant sunburst bordered by toy balloons. Gaudí's plan for the church calls for eight more of these spires, but whether they will ever be built is a matter for history, and Barcelona, to decide.

It was Gaudí's desire to re-create Gothic art, but in a context inspired by the rich flowering of Catalan art at the turn of the century. The artist worked more as a sculptor than as an architect. He changed his ideas often as the work went on, molding huge masses of material with the freedom and exuberance of a child building a sand castle.

The Sagrada Familia's existing facade, which portrays events connected with the birth of Christ, seems literally to grow from the pavement. Stone vines climb upward to provide niches for statues of Biblical characters. What in a regular church would be a pillar becomes a tree in Gaudí's structure. The artist's love of nature is everywhere apparent, right down to the families of stone chickens scratching realistically on either side of the main entrance. To Gaudí, religion encompassed all living things.

Each generation of Spanish artists and artisans interprets the Christmas story in its own unique fashion. There is no way to predict, of course, when the next El Greco or Gaudí will emerge. We can only watch, with pleasure, as the Christmas story continues to unfold in Spanish art.

Tiny figures in native costume cultivate a field of growing grass in this charming nacimiento from Asturias.

Spanish Treats

❖

Judias Verdes con Salsa de Tomate
(green beans in tomato sauce)

2 Tbsp. olive oil
2 cloves garlic, crushed
2 lb. (5 cups) green beans, cut into 1" lengths
1½ lb. canned tomatoes (chopped) and juice
1 Tbsp. chopped chives
salt and pepper
1 bay leaf
1 Tbsp. pine nuts
1 Tbsp. lemon juice

Sauté garlic in olive oil for 2 minutes, stirring. Add beans and cook 4 minutes, stirring constantly. Stir in tomatoes with liquid from can and remaining ingredients; bring to a boil, stirring constantly.

Reduce heat to low and simmer 25–30 minutes. Remove and discard bay leaf. Serve at once. Yield: 6 servings.

Medias Lunas de Nueces
(nut crescents)

1⅔ cups flour
½ lb. unsalted butter
1 cup ground walnuts
1 tsp. vanilla
½ cup confectioners' sugar
pinch of salt

Mix the flour and butter together until they form crumbs. Add walnuts, vanilla, salt, and sugar and mix well. If necessary, chill dough about ½ hour or until dough is workable. Preheat oven to 375°. Cut dough into walnut-size pieces and roll each piece to about 3" in length. Shape each piece into a crescent by pulling it into a semicircle.

Place crescents ½" apart on a baking sheet. Bake for 12–15 minutes until lightly browned. Dust with confectioners' sugar while warm. Yield: About 20 crescents.

Left: *Fresh fruit is a popular food in Spain. Many varieties have been adapted to holiday fare.*

Pastel de Navidad
(*Christmas nut cups*)

Pastry sufficient for 1 pie shell

5 eggs
²/₃ cup sugar
5 Tbsp. butter, melted
pinch of salt
1 tsp. vanilla
1 cup chopped walnuts
²/₃ cup raisins

Preheat oven to 375°. Roll pastry thin and cut into 4″ circles. Fit each round into muffin cup and press in gently. Beat eggs until they are light; add sugar and mix well. Add butter, salt, and vanilla; mix well. Combine walnuts and raisins and fill each cup ½ full. Add egg mixture to fill each cup three-quarters. Bake filled cups 20–25 minutes. Yield: 8–12 nut cups.

Compota de Manzanas
(*apple compote*)

6 tart apples,
 cored and quartered
6 Tbsp. sugar
1 cinnamon stick
1 cup water

Combine sugar, cinnamon stick, and water in a saucepan and simmer for 5 minutes. Cut apple quarters in half, add to saucepan, and cook gently until tender, about 15–20 minutes. Remove apples to serving bowl. Simmer syrup 10 minutes and strain over apples. Serve cold. Yield: 6 servings.

Chocolate a la Española
(*Spanish-style hot chocolate*)

½ lb. sweet baker's chocolate
1 quart milk (or ½ milk, ½ water)
2 tsp. cornstarch

Break chocolate into small pieces. Place in saucepan with liquid. Heat slowly, stirring with a whisk, until just before the boiling point. Dissolve cornstarch in a few tablespoons of cold water. Add dissolved cornstarch to chocolate mixture and stir constantly until the liquid thickens. Serve hot in warmed cups. Yield: 6 small or 4 large servings.

Almendrados
(*almond cookies*)

Preheat oven to 325°. Lightly toast almonds; set aside. Beat egg whites until stiff but not dry. Gradually add sugar, beating constantly. After sugar is added, beat 5–8 minutes. Fold in almonds and vanilla. Place by spoonfuls or shape into rings on greased cookie sheet. Bake 17–20 minutes or until cookies just begin to color. Yield: About 3 dozen.

2 cups blanched almonds, finely
 chopped
2 egg whites, room temperature
1 cup sifted confectioners' sugar
1 tsp. vanilla

Flan
(*caramel custard*)

Caramelized sugar:

10 Tbsp. sugar
5 tsp. water

Heat sugar and water in small skillet over medium-high heat, stirring constantly, until sugar is golden. Remove from heat and pour into 6 ovenproof custard cups.

Custard:

3 eggs
3 egg yolks
¼ tsp. grated lemon rind
6 Tbsp. sugar
2½ cups milk

Beat eggs and egg yolks together lightly with a wire whisk. Add lemon rind, sugar, and milk. Pour into the caramelized cups and place cups in pan of hot water. Cook on top of stove over medium heat 1 hour. Preheat oven to 350°. Cook flan 25 minutes or until knife inserted in center comes out clean. Remove from water and cool, then refrigerate. To serve, loosen sides of custard with knife and invert onto dessert dishes. Yield: 6 servings.

Compota de Peras
(*pear compote*)

2 lb. pears
½ lb. sugar
2 cups water
4 oz. red wine
1 cinnamon stick (3 inches)
grated zest of ½ lemon

Peel and core the pears. Place in pot with remaining ingredients and bring to a boil. Cook 10–15 minutes, until the pears are very soft but still hold their shape. Serve warm or at room temperature with some of the cooking syrup. Yield: 4–6 servings.

Mazapán
(*marzipan*)

3 cups whole almonds, blanched and ground
2 cups sugar
1 cup water
2 egg whites, lightly beaten
3–4 Tbsp. confectioners' sugar
1 tsp. vanilla

In a saucepan, heat water and sugar until sugar dissolves and mixture comes to a boil. Let it boil steadily without stirring until the temperature reaches 230°–234° on a candy thermometer. Remove from heat and beat until mixture turns slightly cloudy. Stir in ground almonds, egg whites, and vanilla. Cook over gentle heat for 2–3 minutes or until mixture pulls away from sides of pan. Turn mixture onto a surface that has been sprinkled with some of the confectioners' sugar. Knead the mixture until smooth, working in the rest of the confectioners' sugar. Pull off pieces and roll into balls or olive-shaped pieces. Wrap in foil or wax paper and store in airtight container.

Churros
(*fried pastry*)

1 cup water
½ cup unsalted butter
¼ tsp. salt
1 cup all-purpose flour
4 large eggs
oil for deep frying
confectioners' sugar

In a heavy saucepan, bring water, butter, and salt to full boil. Remove from heat and immediately add the flour all at once, stirring vigorously until the mixture leaves the sides of the pan and forms a ball. Turn mixture into the bowl of an electric mixer and on medium speed, add one egg at a time, beating only until egg is incorporated before adding the next. After adding the last egg, beat for 1 minute more.

If using a pastry bag, fit it with a ½" open star tip. (A cookie press can also be used. It should have a star tip.) Pipe out 5–6" lengths of dough into 2–3" of oil heated to 375°. Fry, turning occasionally, for 3–5 minutes or until golden brown. Drain well and sprinkle with sugar.

Ensalada de Arroz
(*Andalusian rice salad*)

1 cup converted rice
1 tsp. salt
8 Tbsp. olive oil
3 Tbsp. wine vinegar
1 large clove garlic, minced
1 small onion, minced
salt and pepper
1 4-oz. jar whole pimentos
2 Tbsp. chopped parsley
green and black olives for garnish

This cold rice salad is a modern variation on traditional Spanish ingredients. Bring 2 cups of water to a boil. Add salt and rice; cover and cook slowly 20 minutes or until rice is just tender. While the rice is cooking, make vinaigrette sauce by combining the olive oil, vinegar, garlic, and onion. Season to taste with salt and pepper.

Drain the pimentos. Cut 6 narrow strips and set them aside. Finely chop the remaining pimentos. Cool the rice slightly. Add the vinaigrette sauce, chopped pimento, and parsley. Toss gently.

Spoon rice into a serving bowl. When cool, cover and chill thoroughly. Decorate the top with the reserved pimento strips and olives. Yield: 4–6 servings.

Spanish Accents

❖

Nacimiento

The *nacimiento*, or creche, graces almost every Spanish home and church
at Christmastime. We've designed a manger and figures that can be made
from common household materials. Do not be afraid to experiment with
designs and materials of your own. The Spanish have been
doing so for centuries, so successfully that many *nacimientos*
have found their way into museums.

Materials

- Scissors.

- White glue.

- Assortment of about 50 buttons.
Be sure to have some with two
holes to use for faces, and at least
one small, two-holed button for the
baby Jesus.

- Assorted scrap paper, including
gift wrap, old Christmas cards, construction paper, and magazine
pictures.

- Spools in different sizes and small
plastic bottles, about 10–15 total.

- Assorted scrap trims, such as ribbons, lace, yarn, thread, and tinsel.

- Small package of (25) pipe
cleaners.

- Five drinking straws.

- Empty matchbox.

- For the stable, a shopping bag or
large grocery bag with flat bottom,
either brown or printed. You may
also construct a stable from an old
shoebox or gift box covered with
paper.

- Aluminum foil (optional).

- Marking pens (optional).

- Talcum powder or glitter for artificial snow (optional).

- Modeling clay (optional) in earth
colors or assorted colors. Clay may
be either nondrying or drying—see
the label on the package to deter-
mine which is best for your child.

Figures

The most important *nacimiento* figures are the Holy Family, an angel, and the Three Kings. More elaborate nativity scenes feature animals, shepherds, and other figures that often include a washerwoman plying her trade at an artificial river.

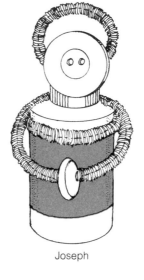

Mary

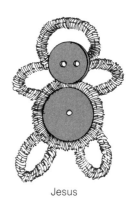

Joseph

Jesus

Three Kings

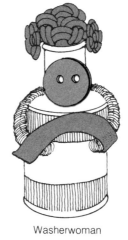

Washerwoman

Angel

Basic construction

A small plastic bottle can serve as the body of any human (or angelic) figure. So can two spools of different sizes, glued end-to-end. Glue and stack buttons on top of the body for halos, crowns, or other headdresses.

buttons

bottle

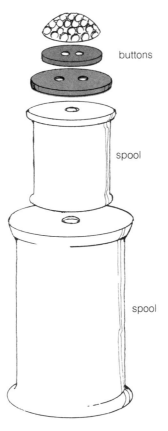

buttons

spool

spool

Cover the body with scrap paper, fabric, or ribbon trimmed to size and glued in place.

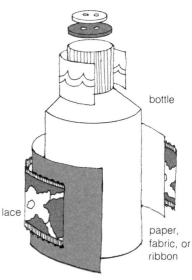

buttons

bottle

lace

paper, fabric, or ribbon

Hands and faces

Buttons with two holes for eyes make good faces. Create noses, mouths, and other features with marking pen, if desired, then glue buttons into place.

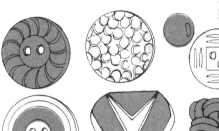

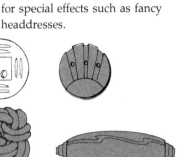

Pipe cleaner arms and button hands complete the figure. Glue pipe cleaner(s) in place at the back of the figure. Glue button hands in place or attach by threading through with pipe cleaner. Hands may hold gifts made of coiled pipe cleaners or buttons glued in place. Fancy buttons—resembling flowers, stars, or spheres, for example—can be used for special effects such as fancy headdresses.

Coiled clay

Many *nacimientos* are made with clay. You can add an authentic touch by decorating figures with coiled modeling clay. Roll thin coils and wrap around figures for decorative crowns and other touches. To make clay arms and hands, twist clay coils around pipe-cleaner arms glued in place at figure's rear.

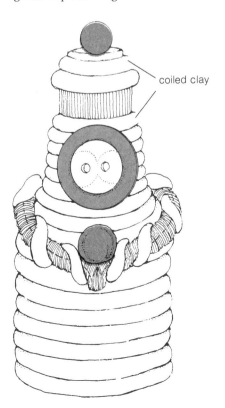

coiled clay

Animal assembly

Four-footed creatures can be made with pipe cleaners and spools. Our fanciful camel begins with a spool body covered with ribbon. Its hump and rear are two or three buttons glued in place on its back. For hoofs, pipe-cleaner legs, twisted around the body's front and rear, are pushed through buttons at the ends. A head-shaped wood button is supported by a pipe-cleaner neck.

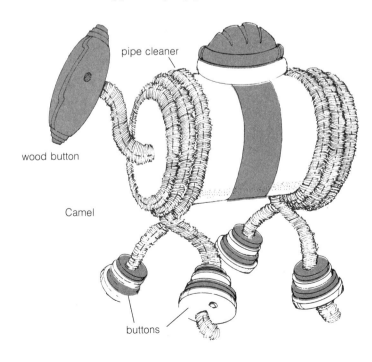

pipe cleaner

wood button

Camel

buttons

Stable

1. Cut a large grocery or shopping bag into three pieces as shown. The bottom of the bag, set on its side, becomes the stable. Snip the stable's four front corners as shown and scallop the front opening.

Fold in the front edges about an inch. Glue the bottom corners as shown.

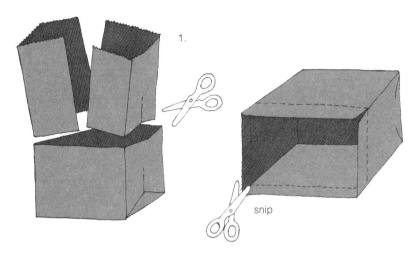

snip

fold and glue

2. Place drinking straws vertically at the four corners of the stable to support your paper-bag building. Make four holes in the roof corners with a sharpened pencil or scissors. Place a drop of glue in each corner of the stable's floor. Insert straws and check to see that they stay in place until the glue is dry. Draw or glue decorations on the outside of the stable. Experiment with strips of colored-paper fringe glued in place along the bottom, sides, or front.

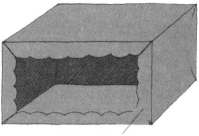

drinking straws

scalloped edge

fringe for grass

3. Make a roof for the stable. Use a leftover piece of your original bag. Fold it fanlike, trim it to size, and decorate to your liking. Glue in place, let the glue dry, and add modeling clay, glitter, or other trim.

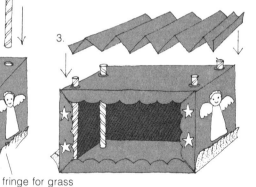

4. Design your stable's interior. Trim the remaining piece of your original bag to fit inside as a pre-folded backdrop. On it draw sheep, cows, windows, or other stable animals and décor. Straw for the stable floor might be tinsel or thin strips of crumpled paper.

5. Make a matchbox manger. Glue both parts of a small, empty matchbox together as shown. Decorate to your liking. Put some "straw" in the manger, and it is ready for the baby Jesus.

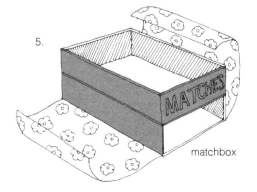

matchbox

Your *nacimiento* can be as simple or elaborate as you wish. Here are some suggestions for authentic Spanish touches.

Mountains

Mountains on either side of the stable can be made from paper bags stuffed with newspaper and crumpled. Top the mountains with tinsel snow. You might also thin some glue with water, paint the mountaintops with glue, and dust them with glitter or talcum powder for snow.

Star

Most *nacimientos* are topped with a Christmas star. Make one from aluminum foil or cut out a pretty star from a Christmas card or magazine. Glue into place at the top of the stable.

Angel

No nativity scene is complete without a Christmas angel. Ours is made from a spool and buttons, with wings cut from a piece of paper folded, fanlike, and glued in place at the back.

wings

Scroll

Most Spanish nativities feature a scroll bearing the words, "Glory to God in the highest, and on earth peace to men of good will." You can create a scroll effect by rolling a strip of paper around a pencil at both ends.

cut out river

River

If you decide to include a washerwoman at a river, make your river with aluminum foil or a strip of blue paper dusted with glitter.

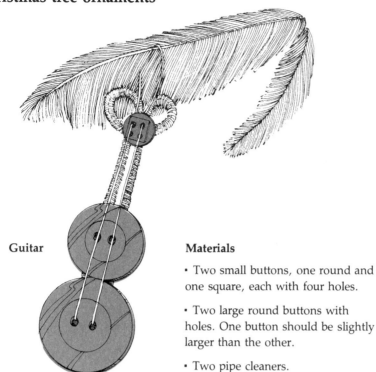

Guitar

Materials

· Two small buttons, one round and one square, each with four holes.

· Two large round buttons with holes. One button should be slightly larger than the other.

· Two pipe cleaners.

· Needle and bright-colored thread.

· Scissors.

· White glue.

· Scrap of yarn or string.

1. Lay out the pipe cleaners side by side and curl the ends, as shown, to form the top of the neck. Thread the needle with a length of thread about three times as long as a pipe cleaner. Knot one end of the thread. Put needle and thread aside for use in step 3.

2. Glue the small square button on top of the small round button, lining up the holes. Glue both to the top of the neck, as shown. The large buttons form the guitar's body. Glue them in place as shown.

3. String your guitar with bright-colored thread before the glue dries on the buttons. Push the needle through the top set of buttons from back to front. Thread through both holes of the large button at the base of the guitar and back up through the top buttons. Secure with a knot at the back. Let the glue dry. Hang your guitar on the Christmas tree by means of a loop made of yarn or string.

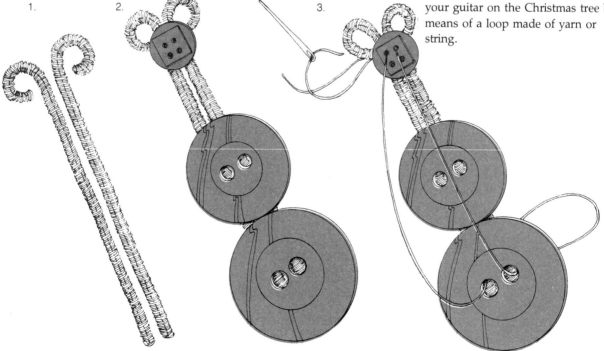

Zambomba

The distinctive sound of a real *zambomba*—a type of drum—is made by moving the center stick up and down through the skin stretched over the top of the drum. Your toy *zambomba* will not make this sound. But the ornament will add an authentic Spanish touch to your Christmas tree.

Materials

· Paper or plastic drinking cup, preferably with lid.

· Sheet of construction paper (if your cup has no lid).

· Scraps of Christmas wrapping paper.

· Drinking straw.

· Three pipe cleaners.

· White glue.

· Scissors.

· Pencil.

· Rubber band.

1. If your cup has no lid, make one from construction paper. Place the top rim of the cup on a sheet of construction paper and trace around it. Then trace another circle around the first, adding a half-inch allowance all the way around. Cut out the larger circle. Clip the edges as shown and fold in toward the center.

2. Glue the lid in place. Fasten it with a rubber band until the glue is dry.

3. Cut a few strips of various wrapping papers. Make them long enough to encircle the cup and overlap at the edges. Smear a thin coat of glue on the sides of the cup and cover the cup with the colored paper. Extra glue may be needed for the overlapping edges. Let the glue dry.

4. Cut two strips of fringed paper long enough to overlap around the top of the cup. Curl the fringe with a pencil. Glue the fringed strips into place, and let the glue dry.

5. With sharpened pencil or scissors, punch three holes in the lid of your cup, as shown—one in the center, and a pair of holes about an inch apart near the edge. Cut a six-inch length of drinking straw. Place a drop of glue on the center hole of the lid. Insert the straw through the hole so that about four inches of straw protrude above the lid. Let the glue dry. As decoration, coil a pipe cleaner or two around the straw. Bend a pipe cleaner to form a loop for hanging the ornament. Put a drop of glue on each of the remaining holes in the lid. Push the ends of the pipe cleaner through the holes and let the glue dry.

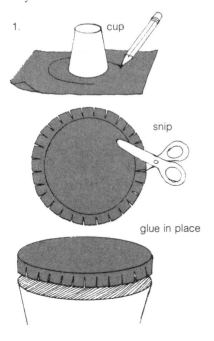

1.

cup

snip

glue in place

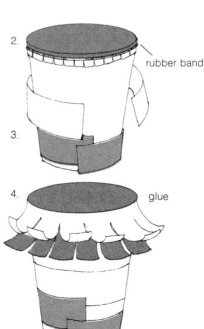

2.

rubber band

3.

4.

glue

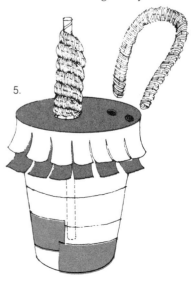

5.

Spanish Melodies

The Son of Mary
(El Noi de la Mare)

Traditional Spanish [GKE]

Traditional Catalonian Carol [WE]

1. Qué li da - rem a n'el Noi de la Ma - re? Qué li da - rem que li
1. What shall we give to the Son of the Vir - gin? What can we give that the

sá - pi - ga bon? Li da - rem pan - ses en u - nes ba - lan - ces,
Babe will en - joy? First, we shall give Him a tray full of rai - sins,

2. What shall we give the Beloved of Mary?
   What can we give to her beautiful Child?
   Raisins and olives and nutmeats and
      honey,
   Candy and figs and some cheese that is
      mild.
   Raisins and olives and nutmeats and
      honey,
   Candy and figs and some cheese that is
      mild.

3. What shall we do if the figs are not
      ripened?
   What shall we do if the figs are still green?
   We shall not fret; if they're not ripe for
      Easter,
   On a Palm Sunday, ripe figs will be seen.
   We shall not fret; if they're not ripe for
      Easter,
   On a Palm Sunday, ripe figs will be seen.

A Fire Is Started in Bethlehem
(En Belén Tocan a Fuego)

Traditional Castilian [GKE]

Traditional Castilian Carol [WE]

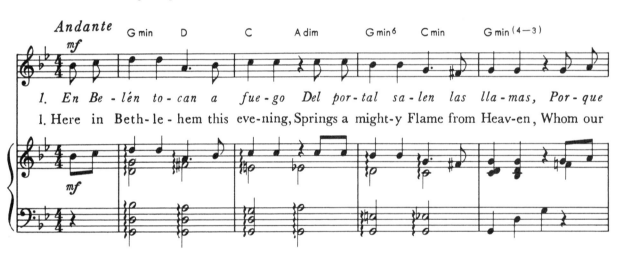

Andante

1. En Be - lén to - can a fue - go Del por - tal sa - len las lla - mas, Por - que

1. Here in Beth - le - hem this eve - ning, Springs a might - y Flame from Heav - en, Whom our

di - cen que ha___ na - ci - do El Re - den - tor de las al - mas.

sin - ful - ness will be con - sum - ing, And through Whom we are for - giv - en.

Allegro
REFRAIN

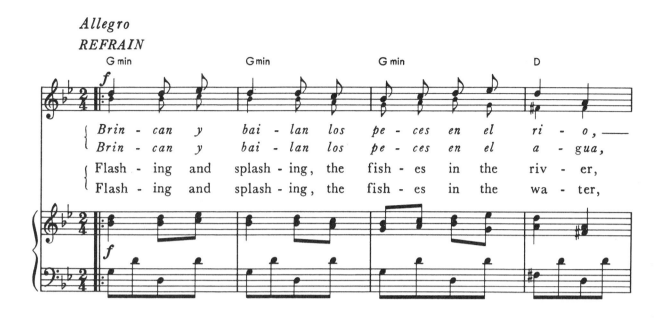

Brin - can   y   bai - lan   los   pe - ces   en   el   ri - o, ____
Brin - can   y   bai - lan   los   pe - ces   en   el   a - gua,
Flash - ing   and   splash - ing,   the   fish - es   in   the   riv - er,
Flash - ing   and   splash - ing,   the   fish - es   in   the   wa - ter,

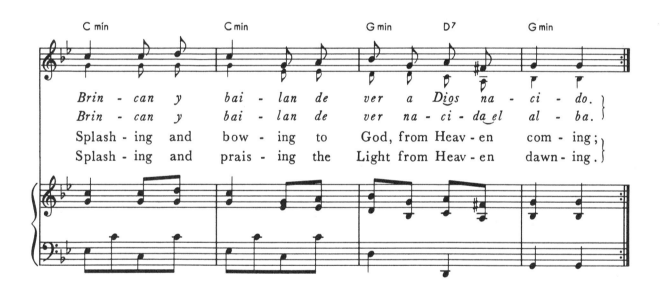

Brin - can   y   bai - lan   de   ver   a   Dios   na - ci - do.
Brin - can   y   bai - lan   de   ver   na - ci - da el   al - ba.
Splash - ing   and   bow - ing   to   God, from Heav - en   com - ing;
Splash - ing   and   prais - ing   the   Light from Heav - en   dawn - ing.

2. In a cold and humble stable,
   Blooms a spotless white Carnation,
   That becomes a lovely purple Lily,
   Sacrificed for our redemption.
        Refrain

3. Washing swaddling clothes for Jesus,
   Mary by a stream is singing.
   Birdlings chirp to her a joyful greeting,
   And the rippling brook is laughing.
        Refrain

Acknowledgments

Cover: WORLD BOOK photo by Steve Hale
2:   © Jadwiga Lopez
6:   © M. Valle, Salmer Arte
7:   Spanish Tourist Office
8:   © Jadwiga Lopez
9:   © Jadwiga Lopez
10:   © C. Zamora, Fotomax
11:   © Maxine Hesse, Fotomax
12:   © J. Buesa, Salmer Arte
13:   EFE Grafica
14:   (Top) Spanish Tourist Office
     (Bottom) © Maxine Hesse, Fotomax
16:   Salmer Arte
17:   © Jadwiga Lopez
19:   © Jadwiga Lopez
20:   EFE Grafica
21:   © Jadwiga Lopez
22:   © Jadwiga Lopez
24:   Salmer Arte
25:   © Jadwiga Lopez
26:   © Maxine Hesse, Fotomax
27:   © Maxine Hesse, Fotomax
28:   (Top) EFE Grafica
     (Bottom) © Jadwiga Lopez
30:   © J. Buesa, Salmer Arte
31:   © Jadwiga Lopez
32:   Hirmer Verlag
33:   Spanish Tourist Office
34:   © Jadwiga Lopez
35:   © Maxine Hesse, Fotomax
36:   Salmer Arte

37:   © C. Zamora, Fotomax
38:   EFE Grafica
39:   EFE Grafica
40:   © Jadwiga Lopez
41:   © Jadwiga Lopez
42:   EFE Grafica
43:   © Jadwiga Lopez
44:   © Jadwiga Lopez
45:   © C. Zamora, Fotomax
47:   EFE Grafica
48:   MAS
49:   WORLD BOOK photo by Steve Hale
51:   Salmer Arte
52:   Salmer Arte
53:   Salmer Arte
54:   Spanish Tourist Office
55:   WORLD BOOK photo by Steve Hale
56:   MAS
57:   Spanish Tourist Office
58:   (Top) Museum of the Art of Catalonia,
     Barcelona; Giraudon
     (Middle) Museum of the Art of Catalonia,
     Barcelona; Giraudon
     (Bottom) Galdiano Museum, Madrid; Giraudon
60:   The Prado, Madrid; Giraudon
61:   The Prado, Madrid; Giraudon
62:   National Museum of Decorative Art, Madrid;
     MAS
63:   National Museum of Decorative Art, Madrid;
     MAS
64:   © Jadwiga Lopez